THE
FATE
OF
THE
MAINE

John Edward Weems

illustrated with photographs

HENRY HOLT AND COMPANY • NEW YORK

The author wishes to acknowledge permission to quote from:

Admirals of American Empire by Richard S. West Jr. Copyright
1948, used by special permission of the publishers, The Bobbs-
Merrill Company, Inc.

"The Battleship *Maine* and Pier 46, East River," by Arthur M.
Johnson, published in U. S. Naval Institute *Proceedings*, November, 1955. Copyright 1955 U. S. Naval Institute.

Two Reels and a Crank by Albert E. Smith and Phil A. Koury.
Copyright 1952 by Albert E. Smith. Reprinted by permission of
Doubleday & Co. Inc.

W. R. Hearst by John K. Winkler. Copyright 1928, used by permission of the publisher, Simon and Schuster, Inc.

89277–0218
Printed in the United States of America

For Jane

Foreword

The United States battleship *Maine* exploded and sank in Spanish-held Havana Harbor on the night of February 15, 1898, and the nation had a battle cry for a war that probably would have been fought anyway: "Remember the *Maine!*"

The ship had been sent to Havana three weeks earlier, ostensibly "to resume the friendly naval visits at Cuban ports," as the State Department said. Actually the *Maine* was sent to protect United States citizens, supposedly endangered by the increasing friction between the United States and Spain.

When the *Maine* blew up, most Americans held Spain responsible, although the evidence was never sufficient to affix blame officially. Some two months later came the Spanish-American War, which was to mark the final collapse of the Spanish Empire and the emergence of the United States as a world power, a rank it has held to this day. Cuba, Guam, the Philippine Archipelago, Puerto Rico, and all other Spanish islands in the West Indies were ceded to the United States, which then entertained fond hopes for an empire of its own.

A glance backward will show that many persons in the United States, including some influential men in government and several important newspaper officials, desired the war.

One of them was Theodore Roosevelt, soon to be Assistant Secretary of the Navy, who said in 1896: "I do not think a war with Spain would be serious enough to cause much strain on the country or much interruption to the revival of prosperity, but I certainly wish the matter could be settled this winter."

Two years later, publisher William Randolph Hearst reportedly wired illustrator Frederic Remington, when Remington sought permission to return home from Cuba in March of 1898: "Please remain. You furnish the pictures and I'll furnish the war."

The reason given by most Americans who wanted war was, oddly enough, to put a stop to the bloody fighting between Spanish forces and insurgents in Cuba, so close to our mainland. But several newspaper publishers, among them Hearst and Joseph Pulitzer, reflected on the possibilities of boosting circulation with a war; and some other important Americans were openly covetous of Spanish-held territory. The cession of land by Spain as a price for ending the war was largely a result of the latter mood, although the United States did pay Spain $20,000,000 for the Philippines. After defeating Spanish arms in those islands, however, the United States found itself fighting island natives to keep the newly won land.

Since the unfortunate ship that blew up in Havana Harbor was so closely linked with a war in which the United States seemed to abandon announced ideals of liberty for all, why, then, remember the *Maine* now?

Let Captain Charles D. Sigsbee, the commanding officer of the *Maine* at the time of the explosion, tell you:

"We have heard much of the motto, 'Remember the *Maine*.' If we are satisfied that the *Maine* was blown up from the outside we have a right to remember her with indignation; but without more conclusive evidence than we now have [1899] we are not right if we charge criminality to persons. Therefore I conceive that the motto, 'Remem-

ber the *Maine*,' used as a war cry [was not] justifiable. . . .
Improperly applied, the motto . . . savors too much of
revenge, too much of evil for evil; but it may be used in an
entirely worthy sense.

"During the recent war with Spain about seventy-five
men were killed and wounded in the United States Navy.
Only seventeen* were killed. On board the *Maine* 252 men
were killed outright and eight died later*—nearly fifteen
times as many as were killed in the United States Navy by
the Spanish land and naval forces during the entire war. In
the way that the men of the *Maine* died and suffered there
was enough of the heroic to provide a sound foundation for
the motto, 'Remember the *Maine*.' "

This, then, is the story of that ship and of the crew who
manned her. The goal has been to present, for a generation
that has forgotten the *Maine*, a true but exciting account of
a ship that has played a most prominent role in the pages of
American history.

To reconstruct accurately the story of the *Maine*, original documents and material obtained through interviews
with survivors have been relied on whenever possible. Most
of the documents were found in the National Archives,
Navy Department Library, and Library of Congress; a
complete list of primary and secondary sources appears in
the Acknowledgments section of this book. Special care has
been exercised in the use of direct quotations; authority can
be cited for every quotation used.

JOHN EDWARD WEEMS

February, 1958

* *Some other authorities give slightly different figures.*

Contents

THE
FATE
OF
THE
MAINE

1

A Ship for the New Navy

The first [United States] battleship of importance was
the U.S.S. "Maine," authorized by act of Congress of
August 3, 1886.

—Joseph Nathan Kane
in *Famous First Facts*

Apprentice Ambrose Ham of Schenectady, New York,
stood chin up, chest out, and prepared to observe, with
scant interest, the commissioning ceremony of the U.S.S.
Maine. With several other bluejackets standing in front
of him, and with a detachment of marines formed in
front of the sailors, he could scarcely see or hear what was
going on anyway.

Ham and the other enlisted men stood on the port side
of the quarter-deck of the fleet's new warship. Facing
them, on the starboard quarter-deck, were thirty blue-
clad officers assigned to the ship. Between the two groups
Ham caught occasional glimpses of the gaunt figure of

Captain A. S. Crowninshield, U. S. Navy, and another naval officer, Captain Frederic Rodgers of the New York Navy Yard, where the *Maine* had been built and was this minute being commissioned. Rodgers was present to turn over the ship to her first commanding officer.

The time was two o'clock in the pleasant afternoon of Tuesday, September 17, 1895.

Ham, a sandy-haired seventeen-year-old with blue-gray eyes, was already a disciplined sailor, but he could not resist musing on some of the absurdities of naval tradition. Here, he thought, was an example. Look at the working time wasted for the ceremony: the crew of the *Maine* had been brought aboard from the receiving ship *Vermont*, where the men were berthed, shortly after noon. They had had nothing to do then but wait until the ceremony began at two o'clock. (Only minutes before two o'clock, Ham's enlisted eye noted, the last of the officers arrived.) Two or three idle hours times the 346 men in the crew added up. But, despite his thoughts, Ham held his five-foot six-inch, 147-pound frame erect, in the proud naval tradition.

Ham and the ship he was helping to put into commission were products of a naval expansion program begun in the early 1880s. After the Civil War had ended, a weary United States citizenry let its navy wither; during a twenty-year period following the war only a few steam sloops and one or two other vessels were built. Most of the naval cash had been spent on repairing antiquated vessels that had been in commission for years, and as these ships aged their repairs had become more expensive.

United States policy then had been to let foreign navies spend money constructing new ships. The designs, officials reasoned, soon would become outmoded anyway, and newer vessels would have to be built. If and when we needed ships, the argument went, we could utilize the latest designs in building them.

This policy resulted in saving money, but to some persons it seemed a false economy. Suppose we should find ourselves suddenly involved in a war, they asked, with no time to build any ships? In a day when sea power was of utmost importance, the United States Navy was admittedly inferior to virtually every other navy in the world. It had been, in fact, a joke among seamen of most countries.

A continuing rebellion against Spanish authority in Cuba, only a short distance off the tip of Florida, had given proponents of naval expansion a strong argument. If the United States should become actively involved in the fighting, they pointed out, the nation would need a powerful navy to cope with Spanish sea power.

The fighting in Cuba had broken out in 1868. Until that time, with several minor exceptions, the island had been a Spanish stronghold since its discovery by Columbus in October of 1492.

The '68 rebellion had lasted for ten years. During that period—in 1873—the Spaniards had captured a filibustering vessel, the *Virginius*, fraudulently flying the United States flag and carrying arms to insurgents in Cuba. The captain, James Fry, and fifty-two of the passengers and crew—among them several Americans—were executed.

Many persons in the United States had clamored then for war. But the country was not prepared. The navy was in poor condition, and the army, kept busy subduing Indians, was undermanned. The United States had remained at peace, but the incident helped to emphasize the need for a stronger navy.

In 1881, when Chester Arthur became President, he stated in his first message to Congress, "Every condition of national safety, economy, and honor imperatively demands a thorough rehabilitation of the navy."

Finally, in 1883, Congress began appropriating cash for a new navy, authorizing three protected cruisers and a dispatch boat. In 1886 the *Maine*—which was to be commissioned as an armored cruiser but remembered as a battleship—was authorized, along with the battleship *Texas*. (This was an earlier ship than the *Texas* now kept near Houston as a memorial.)

The keel of the *Maine* was laid on October 17, 1888, six years and eleven months before commissioning, after a violent early-morning thunderstorm had struck the navy yard. Two years and one month later, on November 18, 1890, twenty thousand persons packed the navy yard to see the hull launched.

The night before had been stormy, similar to the weather experienced on the day the keel was laid, and navy officials were fearful that the launching festivities would be ruined.

"The patriarchs of the fleet," a New York reporter wrote, "vainly twisted their heads this way and that in efforts to catch sight of an omen of good. But the prospect at midnight was bad."

Nevertheless, bright sunshine greeted the anxious officials on the morning of launching day. If this was an "omen of good," however, it was to be a short-lived one. The *Maine*, in her two-and-one-half-year commissioned history, was quickly to be considered "an unlucky ship," as a writer for *Review of Reviews* later commented.

As navy officials had hoped, the sunshine brought out the crowd. Carriages and pedestrians, in two separate lines, streamed into the navy yard through the main gate. One important early arrival, however, came by water. The

U.S.S. *Despatch*, slowly threading her way through numerous small craft, steamed alongside a pier and disembarked General John McAllister Schofield and a party of army officers from Governors Island. Although the army men appeared in mufti, Rear Admiral Daniel L. Braine and his party, on the pier to receive them, were attired in full dress, and their gold braid glittered in the morning sunshine.

A detachment of marines swung their pieces to present arms. Red-coated drummer boys rolled off three ruffles. The crowd cheered; the people had forgotten the Civil War, and this display of militarism seemed wonderful to them. Over their cheers sounded a boom from the *Vermont*; it was the first of a fifteen-gun salute for the general.

By eleven o'clock Naval Constructor William L. Mintoyne had assembled a thousand workmen and was supervising the raising of the *Maine*'s hull from the keel blocks into the launching cradle. Mintoyne, a quiet fifty-year-old man who had superintended the laying of the keel and the building of each compartment, was proud of this ship. It was the first United States warship designed by naval architects and built in a government shipyard.

Eighty oaken battering-rams, each manned by six men, drove in wooden wedges on each side of the ways, lifting the giant steel hull slightly. Then navy-yard workmen armed with axes and hammers split out the keel blocks, and the side shores fore and aft were removed. Sole pieces at the bow, one each to port and to starboard, kept the great ship from sliding down the ways.

The hour set for launching was high noon, but by ten o'clock spectators had begun gathering in the yard in the vicinity of the *Maine*. By eleven o'clock the grounds were crowded; shortly before noon they were packed.

The onlookers observed the bow of the *Maine* projecting several feet from under the shoreward end of a giant shiphouse under which the hull had been built. This gave the vessel the appearance of already having outgrown the expectations of its sponsors. The *Maine* was, however, otherwise unimposing. The ship carried no superstructure or guns yet, and the sides of the hull were still painted a gaudy red.

A few minutes before noon Secretary of the Navy Benjamin Tracy arrived, and a sailor ran his flag to the peak of a navy-yard staff. The *Vermont* this time fired a salute of nineteen guns, and the thrilled crowd roared approval. Tracy raised his hat to return the greeting as his carriage proceeded slowly from the main gate to the vicinity of the *Maine*. There the Secretary ascended steps to a raised, flag-draped platform at the bow of the vessel.

Accompanying Tracy up the steps were several other notables, among them former Secretary of the Navy William Whitney. The crowd cheered them all.

Tracy's young granddaughter, Miss Alice Wilmerding, attracted much attention as she walked composedly toward the platform, taking the rifle salute of the marine guard as if she were used to such heraldry. As she ascended the steps, one woman in the crowd whispered to a friend, "I'm glad she's a girl. If she were older she would be thinking of how she looked and make a mess of it."

Flood tide had been due at 11:57 A.M. that day—launching time had been scheduled to take advantage of it—but a fresh northwester, blowing offshore out of a blue sky flecked with white clouds, delayed it until one o'clock. Shortly after twelve o'clock, however, final preparations were begun for giving the *Maine* her first salt-water bath.

About forty-five minutes after the hour scheduled for the launching, Naval Constructor Mintoyne shouted to the foremen who supervised the thousand yard workmen standing by.

"All clear there?"

"All clear, sir."

"Let her go, then."

Men with saws went to work on the two wooden beams braced against the sides of the bow, and Miss Wilmerding tightened her grip on a bottle of champagne made from grapes grown in San Bernardino County, California. Enmeshed in gold net, with red, white, and blue ribands twined about its neck, the bottle was much too pretty, she thought, to be offered upon the shrine of so unfeeling a monster.

For two minutes the saws gnawed into wood, and nothing happened. Then, at 12:48 P.M. that November 18, 1890, the *Maine* began sliding down the ways.

Secretary Tracy whispered to his granddaughter, "Now, Alice," and Miss Wilmerding raised her arm with a quick movement that tossed her long braid of hair to one side.

"I christen thee *Maine*," she called out in a girlish voice, and she smashed the bottle against the hull. Champagne spattered her white skirt and sprayed over Secretary Tracy and former Secretary Whitney. The two men raised their hats in salute as the ship rumbled toward the water.

It gained momentum rather quickly; the ways had been coated with five thousand pounds of tallow, soap, and oil. Fireworks popped. The crowd saw two men on the deck of the hull hurriedly raise a flagstaff and unfurl an American flag; the ceiling of the shiphouse had prevented erecting a staff earlier.

Two and one half minutes after the ship had begun moving, it rested in Wallabout Channel with "no list, no strain, no scars." The tugs *Nina* and *Catalpa* ran alongside the *Maine* when the vessel had become still in the water. They fetched it alongside a wharf.

After the launching, almost five years had been required to make the *Maine* ready for commissioning. She had had to wait three years just for her American-built armor to be completed. During that time Ambrose Ham had joined the navy, which was expanding in personnel as well as in ships after its post-Civil War decline.

"July 31, 1894," Ham had written in his personal log, a record of his life in the navy that was later to encompass the entire commissioned history of the *Maine*. "Enlisted on board U.S.S. *Minnesota* as an apprentice third class, pay of said rate nine dollars per month. The above named ship was then made fast to the dock at the foot of West 50th St., New York City.

"Was given outfit of clothing and hammock, then sent to the barber, who cut my hair all off, showed the bath tub to me, and informed me to take a bath and put on the uniform. I did, and not being accustomed to blue flannel underclothes and canvas suit I felt rather mean for several days."

But the most difficult part of navy life for young Ham to accustom himself to had been sleeping in a hammock. He could not get to sleep for a long time, and there were several nights when Ham wished with all his heart that he were back on the farm near Schenectady with his father, his sister, and his brother. This was an understandable desire; for Ham, who had quit school at fourteen, was only sixteen when he joined the navy.

In those days sixteen was a legal enlistment age. Boys over the age of fourteen could sign as apprentices and remain in that rate until they reached the age of twenty-one, when they were to be discharged or re-enlisted in a higher rate. When the time came for a decision, most chose to take the discharge.

The rigorous training schedule left Ham little time to be homesick. At the Newport, Rhode Island, training station, where he and the other new apprentices were sent from the *Minnesota*, reveille was rudely sounded at five o'clock every morning. After the unwelcome bugle had blasted them awake, they lashed their hammocks, put them away in lockers, and gulped the cocoa that was doled out.

At 5:30 they scrubbed floors with hot water; then they scrubbed their clothes. After that, under orders to wash faces and necks every morning, the boys scrubbed themselves.

At seven o'clock came lice inspection. The apprentices mustered, took off their shirts, and turned them inside out for the inspecting officer. Finally, at 7:30 A.M., mess call was sounded. Breakfast! Ham and most of the other neophyte sailors were hungry after waiting two and one half hours for the morning meal.

Quarters for muster came at nine o'clock: roll call and more inspection. Then drill, drill, drill, broken only by occasional orders to sweep floors and by the noon and evening meals. At 7:30 P.M. hammocks were served out, and after such a busy day the apprentices usually wasted no time getting into them, although the bugler did not sound taps until 9:05 P.M.

After several weeks of following this schedule it was no wonder that Ham and his young friends rejoiced when the training ship *Essex* arrived at Newport on January 12, 1895. This meant that a training cruise and shore liberty were in the offing. The boys had been allowed no liberty at all at the training station, where even such pleasures as smoking had been prohibited.

On the *Essex*, Ham and the other apprentices made a cruise to several exotic foreign ports. Then, on July 25, 1895, Ham was ordered to the U.S.S. *Vermont*, an old wooden vessel, still in service at that time as a receiving ship. On the *Vermont*, Ham discovered that he was to be transferred to the new ship *Maine*.

Now, on September 17, 1895—more than a year after Ham had enlisted—he stood erect as the commissioning ceremony of the *Maine* progressed. He heard Captain Crowninshield read his orders to the command of the "U. S. Steel Armored Cruiser *Maine*, first rate." Then Ham heard him add some words of his own:

"I expect every man to do his duty."

Ham observed, without raising his head noticeably, that the pennant had been broken at the main truck. Astern, the national ensign, with forty-five stars, hung limply in a slight breeze.

The *Maine* now was an active ship. Ham wrote later in his own log:

"Sept. 17th, 1895. The U.S.S. *Maine* was put in commission and I was one of her crew. We did not eat or sleep on board until the 21st. Every day we would march over to the ship, work until meal hour, then go back to the *Vermont* for our meals. After supper we stayed and slept aboard the receiving ship. On the 21st we took our bag and hammock and went aboard the *Maine* for good."

And there Ham was to stay, until one night in the harbor at Havana, Cuba, two and a half years away.

2

With the North Atlantic Squadron

The *Maine*'s armor belt [is] particularly strong in the region of the water line. This insures immunity against heavy projectiles making an opening where the water can rush in.

—*New York Times*

The weeks after commissioning were busy ones. The *Maine* was not at all ready for sea. Stores had to be loaded and ammunition taken aboard. Ambrose Ham, who was in most of the working parties, discovered that he had little time to become intimately acquainted with the new ship, but when he did have time to observe he marveled, for the *Maine* now was indeed an imposing sight. The once-red hull had been painted a glittering white, as had the bower anchors—which weighed an impressive 9,000 pounds each and were linked to a ten-ton cable—and the boats. The superstructure, funnels, and masts were ocher; guns and searchlights were black. The pilothouse was of varnished mahogany.

Several decades later the *Maine* would have been dwarfed by warships of the fleet, but in her day she was formidable: 324 feet long, 27 feet at the beam, 6,650 tons displacement. The indicated horsepower, 9,290, gave a trial speed of 17.45 knots, although 9.3 was the most economical. Cost of building was $2,500,000. At commissioning, the ship's complement included 31 officers and 346 men, a total of 377.

(Compare these figures with those for modern American battleships like the *Iowa:* 887 feet long, 108 feet at the beam, 45,000 tons displacement. The shaft horsepower, 200,000, gave a reported speed of 33 knots on a trial run. Cost of building was $110,000,000. Wartime complement for the *Iowa* includes 2,700 officers and men.)

The *Maine* carried four ten-inch guns, two each in a forward and an after turret. The forward turret was built on the starboard side, so that it actually extended a few feet over the side of the ship; the after turret was similarly arranged on the port side—an arrangement that gave the guns an unobstructed fire through an angle of 180 degrees on their respective sides and through an angle of sixty-four degrees on the opposite sides. In addition to those guns the ship mounted six six-inch breech-loading rifles, seven six-pounder rapid-fire guns, eight one-pounders, and four Gatling machine guns. There were tubes for four torpedoes.

Ham soon became familiar with the location of the guns, but he was unable to study the rest of the ship closely during the first few days.

The loading of stores continued, and to the young apprentice it seemed that this work would never end. Provisions for officers and crew, in addition to hundreds of pounds of supplies of a more permanent nature that the new ship required, had to be brought aboard nearly every day. Most of the goods were carried aboard by Ham and the other sailors.

"It took nearly two weeks to get things straightened proper," Ham wrote in his log. "After everything was put aboard, including coal, it was found that the ship drew three feet more forward than aft. Some mistake in the plan of stowing stores had been made." To correct this, some weeks later, forty-eight tons of kentledge and cement were taken aboard and stowed at the bottom of the ship, aft.

Ham was not the only person aboard who had looked forward to the day when the initial loading would be completed. John P. Chidwick, the Catholic chaplain of the *Maine,* was in a state of depression at this time.

Chidwick had left Saint Stephen's Church in New York City for naval service a short time before the *Maine* went into commission, and he had looked forward to the new duty with eagerness. Now, however, he was almost sorry he had made the change.

"Everyone seemed busy but me," he reminisced years afterward. "The men were busy, and beyond Sunday mass there was nothing for me to do."

Chidwick's training at Manhattan College, where he had graduated in 1883, and Saint Joseph's Seminary, where he had finished in 1887, seemed wasted now. He sat glumly in his room during the busy post-commissioning days and even considered resigning.

Other officers were having their problems too, but of a severer nature. The chief engineer was concerned about the dynamo. On the night of September 20 his black gang had to shut it down because of excessive heat. Nine days later the bearings became overheated, and the dynamo stopped. The trouble was to recur frequently during the next few weeks. Later the chief engineer also discovered that the revolution indicator would not function.

Another problem, perhaps more customary, was that of maintaining discipline. With the ship tied up at a pier, liberty was frequent; and more than a few sailors found the attractions of the Brooklyn belles and bars too much to ignore. In those days virtually every seaport city had a red-light district; too, alcoholic beverages were sold to anybody—of age or not. On October 2 and 3, thirteen crewmen were absent over leave. Shortly after that the absentee list grew to such proportions that liberty for the crew was stopped.

But the problem of maintaining discipline did not end there. The log of the *Maine* for this period records the fact that C. E. Mitchell was sentenced to bread and water for two days for befouling a deck bucket and that Owen Sheridan was slapped with one month of extra duty for spitting tobacco on deck. In a more serious vein, T. Riordan was arrested while drunk and placed in double irons to await investigation, and Harry Auchenbach was demoted two classes for throwing a man, later rescued, overboard. Although Auchenbach suffered relatively lightly for his misdeed, another sailor, J. J. Brown, was sentenced to a one-year confinement and dishonorable discharge for threatening the officer of the deck.

Still another problem was that of training and welding into one unit the new crew. The commissioning personnel were just beginning to work efficiently as a team when a new draft of seventeen men reported aboard October 7.

In this group was Gustave J. Dressler, who, sixty-two years after he reported aboard the *Maine*, was to remember her fondly as "a good ship."

Dressler, born in Germany, had been only three when his parents moved to the United States. Their ship had docked at New York on the day President James Garfield was shot in Washington—July 2, 1881.

In 1893, at the age of fifteen, Dressler had enlisted in the navy at nine dollars a month. But by 1895 he had advanced to apprentice second class, and he now felt comparatively wealthy with fifteen dollars a month.

Finally, on a hazy November 5, 1895, the ship went out on her own. Ensign (soon to be Lieutenant) Friend W. Jenkins was officer of the deck that morning.

"Eight A.M. to meridian," he wrote in the log after his watch had ended. "Made preparations for getting ship under way. Draft 22 feet 1 inch forward, 21 feet 7 inches aft. [Thus the *Maine*, when loaded and ready for sea, was still still down by the head.] Called all hands; unmoored at 9:45 A.M. Cast off from coal wharf at 9:55 and stood down East River and New York Bay, pilot conning."

Less than two hours later the steam steering gear of the *Maine* became disabled, and the hand gear was coupled up. Steering was then accomplished by using the hand wheel and the two engines, until the *Maine* anchored at 12:40 P.M. in Sandy Hook Bay and repairs were made. The *Maine* had begun steaming toward her destiny with a misfortune that was later to seem characteristic.

During those first few days of steaming, the officers and crew were employed in trying out equipment, swinging ship, firing guns, and other heavy work. Then, on November 16, 1895, the *Maine* anchored away from the New York area for the first time. It was at Newport, Rhode Island, where the great white ship dropped anchor at 11:45 A.M.

"I remembered everything that I went through at this

place," wrote Ambrose Ham, "and I was glad that I was on a cruising ship."

But the *Maine* soon moved again, away from the site of Ham's recruit training.

A light snow, gently carried earthward by a slight northeast breeze, hit the steel bulkheads and wooden decks of the *Maine* and left them moist as the ship stood into Portland Harbor early on the morning of November 25, 1895. This was to be an official visit; the Navy Department had ordered the vessel there so that the proud residents of the State of Maine could pay homage to their favorite ship.

The next day Governor Henry B. Cleaves and James Baxter, mayor of Portland, visited aboard, and the officers received them in frock coats and epaulets. That afternoon, at ceremonies in the hall of the Portland City Building, a group of Maine citizens presented a thousand-dollar silver service to officers of the ship—a soup tureen and two side dishes of sterling silver, "handsomely ornamented with silver pine crosses and needles," as Captain Crowninshield described them. At other ports, ships ordinarily were given a punch bowl and goblets, but Maine was a prohibition state.

"I went ashore once," Ambrose Ham wrote in his log, "but I did not enjoy the liberty, as it snowed most of the time."

On November 28 the *Maine* received civilian visitors, and at 6:50 A.M. on November 29 the ship was under way again for Newport.

A board of inspection had been scheduled to look at the *Maine* when she first visited the Rhode Island base, but the inspection had been delayed, and the ship had proceeded to Portland. Now, however, the board, under a naval captain named George B. Dewey, was ready for its inspection—on a Sunday. This precipitated the first and only crossing Chaplain Chidwick ever had with his captain.

Chidwick was below in his room, preparing for Sunday mass, when he heard a knock at his door. He opened the curtain and observed the captain's orderly, who said:

"Chaplain, the captain presents his compliments to you and says that he does not think we shall be able to hold service this morning, owing to the visit of the inspection board."

Chidwick replied just as formally.

"Orderly, present my compliments to the captain and tell him that I can say mass at any time before one o'clock, and that I am certain the men will be willing to forfeit part of their recreation time before dinner to hear it."

In a few minutes the orderly was back. A knock, and the curtains were opened again.

"Chaplain, the captain presents his compliments to you and states that he knows you will have to fast before mass and that it will be too much to ask of you to fast until one o'clock."

Chidwick again addressed the man.

"Orderly, present my compliments to the captain and tell him that I have often fasted until after one o'clock and that I will find it no inconvenience."

Once again the orderly disappeared, and when he returned it was with this message, after the usual knock and opening of curtains.

"Chaplain, the captain presents his compliments to you and states that we will have mass at the regular time."

Chidwick barely managed to hide a smile.

The following months were unexciting. Life aboard the new ship settled into a peacetime routine of drills, watches, work, eat, and sleep. On December 16 the *Maine* had been assigned to the North Atlantic Squadron, but for more than five months the ship remained in the Norfolk area, and for several weeks of that time—in early 1896— she swung to her anchor in Hampton Roads.

Although this visit was generally dull, one morning proved eventful for Ambrose Ham: on April 14, 1896, he was reduced to the second conduct class at captain's mast for tardiness in obeying orders. It was to be the only black mark against his conduct during his entire navy career.

A day or two earlier, Naval Cadet Wat T. Cluverius, while walking through the crew's compartments, had ordered Ham to perform some menial chore. But the call for quarters was due to come in a matter of minutes, and Ham was attempting to tie his neckerchief in a respectable knot.

"Sir," he said, "I have to get ready for inspection."

"You do as you're told," Cluverius answered.

Ham did then, but it was too late. The cadet put him on report.

Although Ham had his inspections for which to prepare, he and the rest of the crew enjoyed no liberty for a period of several weeks because of a smallpox scare ashore. Time passed slowly for the men. To enliven the wait, a ship nearby, the *Columbia*, gave a banquet and a ball, "with plenty of beer and cigars," for the crew of the *Maine*. Fifty sailors went over for the fun.

Then the *Maine* crewmen decided to reciprocate, and each sailor contributed one dollar. Chidwick had charge of the arrangements. The bugler trained a band, and Chidwick assembled talent for a minstrel show. Cooks and stewards planned a grand banquet that was to start with oysters and end with ice cream.

For days before the event was scheduled, tailors aboard the *Maine*—including young Ham, who was quite a hand at sewing and embroidering—worked on costumes and dresses, historical and contemporary. Rope was manipulated into curls for the sailors who would dress as women for the ball. Well-known historical figures, portrayed by costumed sailors, were to take part in the grand march.

On the day of the festivities, the *Maine* was decorated with colorful bunting. The deck was waxed and covered with awnings. Wives and friends of the officers (perhaps immune to smallpox) came aboard early in the afternoon, and by three o'clock the *Columbia* sailors were aboard. The minstrel show began then and lasted until five o'clock.

Next came the food, and after helping themselves to generous shares of the banquet dishes the crew of the *Columbia* repaired to their ship to costume themselves for the ball.

In the grand march, Chidwick recalled, there appeared "ladies from Revolutionary days, Bowery girls with cigars instead of cigarettes, women with washboards and brooms." The dancing lasted until after midnight, and Ham observed that "one or two of our men got drunk and made a good deal of noise but did not stop the fun. Everybody had a splendid time."

Still, it was the concensus among the crew that regular shore liberty was more diverting. They looked forward to the day when it would be resumed.

On June 4, 1896, the *Maine* left the Hampton Roads area and arrived at Key West for a fifty-two-day visit.

After that it shuttled between Hampton Roads and Tompkinsville, New York.

On one visit to the Norfolk Navy Yard the first death aboard the *Maine* occurred. A yard employee, William Cosgrove, who had been discharged from the navy two months previously, walked down the gangway at noon on August 11 after working aboard all morning. A seaman on the gangway watch disinterestedly gazed at Cosgrove making his way to a building for his lunch. Suddenly the sailor was startled to see the worker collapse. He notified the officer of the deck.

Two men hurriedly brought Cosgrove back aboard the *Maine* for medical attention, but he died of a cerebral hemorrhage in a matter of minutes.

After Cosgrove's death, the *Maine* once more made a trip to Tompkinsville. During January and the first few days of February of 1897, however, the ship remained at Hampton Roads. Then, on Thursday, February 4, 1897, it departed on a voyage that few crew members would soon forget.

The morning was cloudy and cold as the *Maine* joined four other vessels of the North Atlantic Squadron in standing out from Hampton Roads. They were bound for Charleston. Storm signals had been displayed ashore even as the ships got under way.

The vessels were formed in column. Four hundred yards ahead of the *Maine*, the flagship *New York* plowed through the water. Four hundred yards astern of the *Maine* steamed the *Indiana;* then followed the *Columbia* and the *Amphitrite*. By early afternoon the bridge personnel of the *Maine* sighted, several miles ahead, another ship, the *Marblehead*, under orders to join the formation.

The *Marblehead* saluted the admiral with thirteen guns. The *New York* answered with seven, the number of guns rated by the captain of the *Marblehead*, and instructed the newcomer to take over number-five position in the column. The *Amphitrite* dropped back to sixth, and the ships steamed into the open Atlantic.

From the bridge of the *Maine*, Captain Crowninshield felt a breeze from the northeast and observed a long, heavy swell coming from the same direction. He needed no other weather signals to tell him that a storm was not far away. He saw the *New York*, still ahead, roll and pitch, and he felt the *Maine* do the same. Although he could not observe so easily the *Indiana* astern, that vessel was laboring more heavily than any of the others.

"This ship," wrote Naval Cadet E. H. Watson in his *Maine* cruise book, "rolled twenty-two degrees on each side of the vertical."

At 8:00 P.M. the *Indiana* signaled the flagship, advising the admiral that her turrets were working loose and that she could not secure them. The admiral immediately replied, ordering the *Indiana* to return to Hampton Roads.

During the night the swell continued to toss the ships, making sleep difficult for those below. Early Friday morning, February 5, the formation ran into the Gulf Stream, and the temperature of the water rose from forty-six to sixty-nine degrees. But this did not herald milder weather. Conditions continued to grow worse, and the vessels rolled and pitched more than ever.

At eight o'clock that morning the *Maine* was off Cape Hatteras, the stormy graveyard of ships. At 9:30 A.M., although the crew was mustered at quarters as usual, Ambrose Ham and several others discovered that it was difficult to keep on their feet; the *Maine* occasionally rolled as much as twenty-five degrees.

During that day Naval Cadet Watson made an additional entry in his cruise book:

"Sea on the quarter and beam. Wind shifted from NE to ENE, then to E by N and to ESE. Force of wind increased almost hourly."

Squalls enveloped the ships during most of the day, and still the storm grew in intensity. The next day—Saturday, February 6—the *Maine* had her closest brush with disaster until the night in Havana one year and nine days later.

Sleepy men roused for the midwatch left their hammocks for a miserable four hours. A strong gale, accompanied by heavy rain, was blowing from the southeast.

No sooner had Lieutenant Carl W. Jungen relieved the officer of the deck at midnight than the *New York* signaled a course change to south seven degrees east, to head the ships into the sea. At 1:00 A.M. the flagship followed this up with an order decreasing speed to four knots. Still the stormy Atlantic pounded the warships and broke over their bows.

When Lieutenant George Blow relieved Jungen as officer of the deck at four o'clock that Saturday morning, Blow was alarmed to observe a still rapidly falling barometer. The wind had increased in force to a heavy gale, and the rain came in sheets. At 4:15 A.M. Blow lost sight of the lights of the *Marblehead*, and at five o'clock the *Columbia* and *Amphitrite* disappeared from his view. He could discern only the lights of the *New York*, about a thousand yards off his starboard bow.

Relieved shortly before eight o'clock, Blow wearily descended the ladder from the bridge and made his way aft to his stateroom. His route led him past the room of Chaplain Chidwick.

Chidwick had been accustomed to waking "rather

early" and to celebrating mass every morning in his room. This morning he was awake as usual, but for a while he simply clung to his bunk, aware of the intensity of the storm. Then he determined to go on deck—never before had he seen a storm at sea. He had almost completed dressing when Lieutenant Blow passed his room.

"This is one of the worst storms I've ever seen," Blow warned.

To the men topside, the storm was frightening indeed. Rolling green seas pounded the ram bow of the *Maine*, and the wind flung incredibly stinging raindrops into the unprotected faces of sailors on watch.

At 8:15 A.M. L. C. Kogel, an apprentice second class, was securing the port accommodation ladder when a heavy sea broke over him and he lost his footing. Charles Hassel, third-class gunner's mate, tried to seize Kogel, but both men were swept overboard by the churning water.

Kogel was immensely popular among the crew members, and one of his best friends, Landsman William Creelman, immediately leaped over the side into the stormy sea in an attempt to rescue him.

Below deck a startled Chaplain Chidwick heard a cry. "Man overboard!"

It was echoed throughout the ship (for in those days there was no public-address system; the only way to pass the word was by shouting).

On the bridge, Lieutenant Jenkins, who had relieved Lieutenant Blow of the deck, immediately ordered two life buoys to be thrown over the side and stopped both engines.

By that time Captain Crowninshield had reached the bridge, and he ordered the starboard engine backed. In a matter of moments—the *Maine* was now a well-disciplined ship—a crew under Naval Cadet W. R. Gherardi had assembled to man the port whaleboat. The *Maine*, however, was rolling and pitching so violently that lowering a boat safely appeared to be impossible.

"It seemed, as the ship rolled, that they would be swamped before they could get away from the side," said Chaplain Chidwick, who by now had reached the main deck. But the boat crew finally managed to clear the ship by a superhuman feat of rowing.

By this time Creelman and Hassel were some distance off the port bow. Kogel had disappeared, drowning within two minutes. Worried sailors watching from the deck saw that Hassel clung to the life buoy while Creelman swam for it in the mountainous waves.

The raging sea carried the whaleboat astern, and Cadet Gherardi discovered that making progress toward Creelman and Hassel was impossible. The battered boat then lost its rudder, but quickly John Herbert of Brooklyn jerked the belt from around his waist and with it lashed an oar to the stern of the boat to keep it heading into the sea.

Chaplain Chidwick prayed silently for the men in the boat when he saw them rise high upon the crests of giant waves, then disappear, "as if under the sea itself."

On the bridge, Crowninshield beckoned to a signal boy and told him to advise the boat crew that they would be taken back aboard. Crowninshield put his helm to port, and during the turn the *Maine* wallowed in the trough of the sea.

The ship rolled as never before. Below decks, as pieces of gear fell out of stowage spaces and clattered and crashed against bulkheads and decks, the noise was almost as terrifying as the movement. It was a wonder that anyone was able to keep on his feet; the *Maine* rolled from forty-two to forty-five degrees, and most of the crew were certain that their ship was capsizing.

"If the ship had rolled five more degrees," Ambrose Ham thought, "she would have kept on going."

Another mountain of water crashed over the vessel. Marine Private A. B. Nelson, clinging for his life on the quarter-deck, was swept into the sea and not seen again. Two men nearby also were knocked off their feet and carried under the water, but they saved themselves by grabbing a deck railing.

From the bridge, Crowninshield shouted over the din of the storm to those below:

"Clear the deck!"

But Chaplain Chidwick hesitated. "For a moment," he said, "I waited to give absolution to the men."

Then Chidwick darted through the hatchway leading to his room. He took off his raincoat; it would only be in the way if he, too, were swept upon the sea. He had just thrown the coat on his bunk when he heard another cry.

"Man overboard!"

This time it was John Brown, a seaman, who had been washed over by another wave before he could reach safety. Brown disappeared as quickly as had Private Nelson.

When Chidwick returned to the deck he noticed the lifeboat alongside. Each roll of the *Maine* seemed certain to smash the craft, but men still on deck hastily lowered ropes to those in the boat and hauled them up. Shortly afterward, the towing hawser that had been secured to the whaleboat parted, and Chidwick saw the boat drift away empty, on the stormy sea.

The captain headed his ship for the spot where he had last seen the buoy and the two men, and a lookout soon shouted:

"They're both ahead, sir, and both on the life buoy."

Anxious crew members, waiting on deck to haul the two aboard, watched as a wave tossed Creelman off the buoy. Hassel grabbed him and pulled him back.

The first attempt to bring the ship near enough for a rescue failed.

"Had a wave swept over the ship at that time," Chidwick recalled later, "it would have swept nearly the full complement overboard." Everyone was on deck, it seemed, with the exception of the engine-room watch.

At 9:25 A.M. Hassel and Creelman finally were hauled aboard, and it was none too soon. A dense mist enveloped the ship and cut visibility to about one hundred feet. Once, it cleared briefly, and the sailors on the *Maine* caught a glimpse of the *Marblehead* plunging deeply. Then the *Marblehead* vanished behind the mist. Soon, some persons on deck heard a crash, like thunder. Their first thought was that the *Marblehead* had foundered in the storm and had fired a gun before going down.

One seaman said to Chidwick, "Chaplain, it sounds like the crash of doom." But when the mist cleared again the men observed that the *Marblehead* was still afloat.

At 11:00 A.M. came the word for the crew to muster at quarters. The tragedy was confirmed, and weary Captain Crowninshield gave an order to the signal boy on watch: "Tell the flagship, 'Three men lost.'" An entry, accordingly, was made in the log: "Found Leonard C. Kogel (app 2c), John Brown (sea), and Axel B. Nelson (pvt, U.S.M.C.) missing."

Chidwick waited a few minutes for the doctor to administer aid to the two men who had been picked up from the water; then he went below to comfort them. He found Creelman—who was later awarded a gold medal for heroism by Secretary of the Navy Tracy—coming out of the sick bay chewing on a pig's foot. Hassel was inside, lying exhausted on the deck. He had injured his back, before he was swept overboard, when the sea threw him against a stanchion. Chidwick was pleased to see that Hassel held a rosary.

The *Maine* was hove to then, with her head to the wind and sea. She rolled heavily at times for the rest of that Saturday and eventually lost sight of the *New York*. By next morning the storm had abated, and she was able to rejoin the *New York* at 7:00 A.M.

About nine o'clock that Sunday night Captain Crowninshield and the officer of the deck thought they heard a cry. They listened, and again they seemed to hear it.

"Stop the engines," ordered the captain. He listened again, carefully, and heard nothing; but he ordered the forward searchlight manned.

As its bright arc cut into the blackness, those on the bridge of the *Maine* scanned the sea. They saw nothing. The captain ordered his engines ahead and put his helm hard to starboard. The *Maine* made a complete circle while the searchlight played over the water.

Nothing.

Crowninshield ordered the ship back on course for Charleston. The mystery was never explained. Probably, Crowninshield and his watch officer thought, their imaginations had been too vivid.

About two weeks after the storm, the *Maine* was ordered to represent the navy, in company with the battleship *Texas*, at New Orleans' famed Mardi Gras carnival. With every man aboard eagerly anticipating the duty, the *Maine* sailed from Port Royal, South Carolina, on February 21. At 7:15 A.M., February 25, the ship took aboard a river pilot at Crescent Station, south of New Orleans.

A driving mist and a stiff breeze from the north dampened the spirits of many watch-standers on deck as the ship moved up the Mississippi River against a fierce, eight-knot current. But Apprentice Ham was determined not to let the weather interfere with his sight-seeing. He stood on the open deck. Although his first impression was somewhat disappointing—the water, he discovered, was "rather muddy"—he still looked forward to catching a glimpse of fabulous New Orleans.

Sometime before five o'clock that afternoon the opportunity came. He saw the city in the distance to port. The harbormaster, having come aboard at 4:30 P.M., helped anchor the white warship at 5:10 in twenty fathoms off the foot of Canal Street, near the Algiers side of the river.

"As we passed up to the city," Ham wrote in his personal log, "all the boats on the river commenced to blow their whistles and sirens, and such a noise they made! It was kept up long after we anchored."

Ahead of the *Maine* lay the French warships *L'Iphigenie* and *Dubordieu,* the latter with a rear admiral on board. The *Maine* saluted with thirteen guns, then made preparations, not for liberty and gaiety, Ham discovered, but for painting the sides of the ship. The very next day the crew turned to on this work.

At 2:50 P.M. that day Ham sighted the *Texas* proceeding slowly up the river to join the *Maine* for the carnival.

"She was welcomed with the enthusiasm we were," he observed.

Soon the *Texas* anchored, and she, too, saluted the French rear admiral.

The anchorage was a poor one, at least during the time the *Maine* and *Texas* were there. The swift river current hurled against the sides of the ships a large amount of debris, kicked up by a flood upstream, and logs damaged the launch and the first whaleboat of the *Maine*.

On Sunday, February 28, visitors flocked to see the two ships. Aboard the *Maine* one sight-seer sprained an ankle and another fainted, but this failed to lessen the enthusiasm. People continued to pack the wharf on the New Orleans side of the river, waiting for boats to the warships.

"This is the first time," the *Daily Picayune* commented, "that New Orleans has ever had the pleasure of greeting an American vessel of such dignified rating as a battleship."

Monday afternoon, March 1, 1897, King Rex came to the city. Earlier, the *Maine* had dressed ship rainbow-style for the occasion. At 1:35 P.M. the *Texas*, then the *Maine*, joined in the gaiety, manning the rail and saluting the arrival of the king of the carnival with twenty-one guns.

Ambrose Ham witnessed the ceremony from the foot of Canal Street, where he waited with a group of *Maine* sailors who were to march in the royal procession to the city hall. He saw King Rex, accompanied by his dukes, army, and attendants, come up the river on the royal yacht, which looked, to Ham, "like a scow." A fleet of vessels gaily decorated with bunting accompanied the yacht.

The king and his court, Ham saw when they had disembarked near where he stood, were masked and dressed in colorful costumes. Along Canal Street an estimated 120,-000 persons jammed balconies, sidewalks, and windows to observe the festivities.

"We fell in line then," Ham wrote later, "and marched to the city hall, where the mayor turned over the keys of the city to King Rex—which meant that the people could do almost as they pleased and not get arrested."

Ham had expected a great deal of the carnival. He had heard about the masked balls, the parades, the tableaux; he had been told that a person could "wander amid birds, butterflies, and flowers, in coral caves under the roots of

the ocean—or amid enchanted forests, where griffins, drag-
ons, and other fabulous beasts held sway." But now he was
disappointed—perhaps he had expected too much. Although Canal Street, with its pennants, flags, and green,
gold, and purple carnival colors prominently displayed,
made a favorable impression on the young sailor as he
marched, he thought that Mardi Gras "was not what it is
cracked up to be. I saw only a couple of persons dressed up
in funny costumes, and a good many of the sailors were arrested."

But many other crew members of the *Maine*, unlike
Ham, thoroughly enjoyed the visit, as Ham's comment
about the number of arrests might indicate. At morning
quarters on March 1, thirty-six men failed to answer at
muster; three men who returned in no condition to answer anyway were placed in the custody of a sentry. Later,
still another sailor was put in double irons for "being
drunk and fighting." Even the officer in charge of the detachment of marines found the lure of New Orleans too
great. He absented himself without leave for several days.
The situation became so bad that Captain Crowninshield
offered a ten-dollar reward for the return of any man who
was overtime.

One day before the ship departed, a group of Maine na-
tives who resided in the Louisiana city came aboard to
present to Crowninshield, for the ship, a nine-inch-high
silver loving cup with moose-horn handles. Then, on
March 11, the *Maine*, following the *Texas*, departed, leaving behind most of a one-month payroll and six crew
members, five of whom had already been declared deser-
ters. It was a five-day trip back to Port Royal.

One month later the *Maine* lay at anchor in Hampton
Roads when a new commanding officer came aboard. He

was Commander Charles D. Sigsbee, a spectacled man who had been in naval service since the age of fourteen but who looked more like a professor than the captain of a warship. As a commanding officer, however, he was efficient—the *Maine* was to be his seventh command—and, in fact, he was a favorite in the Navy Department. As chief of its hydrographic office for four years, he had improved its efficiency to a marked degree.

April 10, 1897, was a big day for Sigsbee. In addition to assuming command of the *Maine*, his commission as captain was signed, and this was at a time when promotions were exceedingly slow. The promotion brought an increase in pay for Sigsbee, from $3,500 annually as a commander to $4,500.

At 1:30 P.M., before the officers and crew mustered aft on the main deck, he took over the ship from the outgoing commanding officer. Crowninshield read aloud his detachment orders; then Sigsbee read orders assigning him to the *Maine*. The afternoon was cool and partly cloudy; a slight north breeze left the colors nearly limp, as on the day of commissioning. Sigsbee must have felt a deep elation on this pleasant day as the impressive warship became his.

Sigsbee was the officer—an intelligent, iron-willed, yet sympathetic one—who was to command the *Maine* into the pages of American history. Within one year he was to have more than one opportunity to test under extreme conditions his service creed: "An officer in emergency should pour ice water over his personal feelings, in order to defer his nervous prostration to a proper moment."

3

Ordered to Cuba

The condition of affairs in Havana is critical and is
likely to continue so. It is the opinion of General Lee
that sooner or later it will be necessary to have one or
more U.S. vessels appear in Havana.

—Captain Charles D. Sigsbee,
in an official letter on January 21, 1898

The *Maine* had her first contact with Spaniards twelve
days after Captain Sigsbee came aboard. On April 22,
1897, the vessel was anchored with other ships of the
North Atlantic Squadron off Tompkinsville, New York,
when, at about 9:00 A.M., the Spanish cruiser *Maria Teresa* appeared on the horizon. The *Teresa*, making an official visit, was bound for a North River anchorage.

Admiral F. M. Bunce, on the *New York*, ordered a signal to the *Maine:* "Board the Spanish man-of-war." This
action, a formality, was meant to be a cordial exchange of
greetings, not a warlike act.

On the *Maine*, the officer of the deck immediately called

away a boat. Another officer embarked in it, and the crew rowed him toward the oncoming *Maria Teresa*. The Spanish ship ignored his hail and continued on course. The *Teresa* did fire a national salute to the United States when she passed through the Narrows, however, and she saluted the admiral. The *New York* returned it gun for gun.

Later that same day—at 6:00 P.M.—still another Spanish cruiser, the *Infanta Isabel*, reached the vicinity of Bunce's ships. Once more the boarding officer from the *Maine* was ignored. He returned stanchly to his ship.

But greater challenges were in store for the personnel of the *Maine*. Three months later, on the morning of July 29, Captain Sigsbee's quick thinking averted what might have been a worse tragedy than the one which was to strike the ship little more than six months later.

The ship had left a Connecticut anchorage the day before and had steamed into Long Island Sound, bound for Tompkinsville. Squalls had cut visibility as night fell, and at midnight the *Maine* had anchored.

Early the next morning the ship got under way again and steamed down the Sound, passing through Hell Gate soon after 9:00 A.M. Moving down the East River on an ebb tide, the *Maine* had put the navy yard astern and by 11:10 A.M. was nearing Brooklyn Bridge. Captain Sigsbee, qualified to be his own pilot because of his coastal survey work, stood on the bridge, having taken the conn from Lieutenant John J. Blandin, officer of the deck.

Coming up the river, Sigsbee observed, was an excursion steamer, the *Chancellor*, flying an Irish flag and filling the air with Irish music—all in honor of members of an Irish organization on board. From the bridge of the *Maine*, the amused Sigsbee watched the approaching steamer with more than professional interest.

The *Maine*, slightly to the left (or Brooklyn) side of the river, was steaming at "ahead slow" on both engines. On the port bow Sigsbee noticed two large railroad barges in tow, also going downriver. On the starboard bow he observed the steamer *Colorado* being towed down the river by a tug.

Sigsbee looked again at the *Chancellor* and saw that the railroad barges appeared to be dangerously close to it. The *Chancellor*, he could see, was trying to pass between the barges and a Brooklyn pier. But suddenly the ship and one of the barges collided. The *Chancellor*, Sigsbee observed, then made for the Brooklyn shore, but she was also still making headway upstream.

The tug towing the railroad barges sheered off to starboard, dead ahead of the *Maine*. The tug towing the *Colorado* also turned to starboard, and the *Colorado* swung broadside to the current. The vessel occupied a large part of the East River.

The barge tug then began backing to clear the *Colorado*, and Sigsbee swung the *Maine* to starboard to clear them both. It was impossible to turn to port, Sigsbee had realized, because of the proximity of the Brooklyn shore and because of the *Chancellor*, still coming up the river in that vicinity.

Into this situation blundered another large excursion steamer, the *Isabel*, carrying eight hundred members of the Alligator Club of Newark. Heading up the river between the *Colorado* and the New York shore, the *Isabel* lay in the path of the *Maine*. Captain Sigsbee saw that if he stayed in the channel he might ram the excursion steamer.

When the passengers on the *Isabel* realized their predicament they became panicky, rushing to the rails in anticipation of having to abandon a sinking ship. The band aboard the steamer, attempting to quiet the crowd, struck up "The Star-Spangled Banner." But Sigsbee, making a split-second decision, rammed Pier 46 instead.

The impact was so great that the *Maine* rebounded from the pier. Sigsbee ordered the collision signal sounded, and all watertight doors were closed, but the warship had sustained only a slight loss of paint and a few dented plates. The captain backed his ship away from the pier and made for the navy yard. When he discovered that the *Maine* was not badly damaged he completed the trip to Tompkinsville, where the ship anchored shortly after midnight.

A group of naval officers investigating the accident pronounced Sigsbee's judgment "sound and correct" and said that he probably avoided a serious disaster and much loss of life by the course he took. Acting Secretary of the Navy Theodore Roosevelt added his own words of praise: "You have reflected credit upon yourself and upon the service to which you belong."

"The story of the *Maine* leading up to the explosion," said Captain Sigsbee in 1899, "may be said to begin at the Southern Drill Ground of the North Atlantic Squadron on October 9, 1897."

In late August seven ships of the squadron—the *New York, Iowa, Brooklyn, Massachusetts, Indiana, Texas,* and *Maine*—had been on maneuvers off the New England coast. From there the squadron, under Rear Admiral Montgomery Sicard, had proceeded to the Southern Drill Ground, about twenty-five miles east of Cape Charles, Virginia, where the ships had "great-gun" practice during the day and occasionally at night.

The squadron had remained at the drill ground for ten days, constantly practicing, when it was ordered into

Hampton Roads for coaling. From the anchorage in the roads one or two ships at a time steamed to Newport News to take on coal.

Then, in the first days of October, 1897, the squadron had got under way for Yorktown, Virginia, where the crews were engaged in boat drills and shore landings. Ambrose Ham participated in a sham battle, with "leggings, rifle, and mess kit," near the site of Washington's victory over Cornwallis in the Revolutionary War.

Ham realized that he was fortunate to be in the navy instead of the army.

"We retreated," he wrote, "at the same time firing our empty rifles and throwing big pieces of dirt. We were chased all over the place. We had to run through sand, and the sun was hot, and the water in our canteens was warm. I was glad when it was all over."

After that the squadron had departed once more for the Southern Drill Ground. It was anchored there on the night of October 8, awaiting the arrival of the *Brooklyn*, which had remained in Hampton Roads to complete some repairs. When the *Brooklyn* rejoined the fleet, all the ships were to proceed to Boston to take part in a celebration. The *Brooklyn*, however, did not arrive that night.

Shortly after midnight men on signal watch in the fleet observed the lights of two approaching vessels; they proved to be the torpedo boats *Dupont* and *Ericsson*. They carried dispatches for Admiral Sicard on the *New York*.

The *Indiana*, Sicard learned, had been ordered to return to Hampton Roads. The *Maine* was to be detached and sent, singly, to Port Royal, South Carolina.

Captain Sigsbee, summoned aboard the flagship for his orders, immediately understood their significance. The United States government, he reasoned, wanted to have a

formidable warship near Havana in the event of out-
breaks against American citizens there.

Relations between the United States and Spain had
been deteriorating for several years. Much of the friction
was caused by the rebellion in Cuba. Spain had accused
the United States of aiding native insurgents on the island; the United States had countered by accusing Spain
of cruelty in attempting to suppress the uprising. Some
American officials believed that unless the chaotic conditions in Cuba were straightened out immediately the
United States should intervene.

More than a few Americans, however, seemed at that
time to want a war with Spain simply for the sake of
fighting. Thirty-three years had elapsed since the end of
the Civil War, and much of the unpleasantness of armed
conflict had been forgotten. Too, the West had been won,
leaving Americans more time to think about problems
other than their own.

The revolt in Cuba, which had begun in 1868, had
faded after ten years. But in 1895 it had flared up again.
To quell the new revolution, General Don Valeriano
Weyler y Nicolau was sent from Spain to take over as
captain general of the island. His methods, which immediately earned him the nickname of "The Butcher" in
American newspapers, were effective enough to bring relative calm in 1897. They also left several hundred thousand Cubans starving.

Then a change of government at Madrid from conserv-
ative to liberal felled Weyler; the liberals had been seeking his recall for several months. Weyler sent his resignation, and a more moderate man, Ramon Blanco, replaced
him in October, 1897, as captain general. Blanco came,
conciliatorily, with a plan for autonomy for Cuba, but by

that time most Cubans were in a mood to settle for nothing less than complete independence.

Still, the United States might have been able to steer clear of future involvement in Spanish-Cuban affairs except for the irresponsible actions of certain groups. Prominent among them were newspapers.

An example appeared in the *New York Journal* early in 1898, when Richard Harding Davis cabled from Havana a dispatch relating how Spanish police had boarded the American steamship *Olivette*, shortly before it sailed for the United States, and searched three young Cuban women. Illustrating the story was a drawing by Frederic Remington, showing three lewd-looking Spaniards stripping one of the girls in her cabin. Over the story a headline screamed: DOES OUR FLAG PROTECT WOMEN?

Most Americans were furious, and many congressmen demanded an immediate investigation. The fact was, it developed much later, that the search had been conducted by a Spanish policewoman, not by three men.

Such incidents kept war fever at a high pitch in the United States, and Spanish officials, now striving to work out a compromise that would avert a costly war yet save face for them, were at an extreme disadvantage. To complicate matters, some Spaniards were no less antagonistic toward the United States; so that by the time Captain Sigsbee received his orders to take the *Maine* to Port Royal the question was not so much whether war could be averted as when it would come.

The *Indiana* left the squadron the same night the orders arrived, but the *Maine*, engaged in some minor repairs (not uncommon work on the ship), did not weigh anchor until the next morning. The ship arrived at Port Royal on October 12 and remained there for more than a month.

"Excepting our pleasant association with friends at the naval station," Captain Sigsbee commented, "we had a dull time."

On the afternoon of November 14 a liberty party had embarked in a boat, at the foot of the gangway ready to shove off, when the officer of the deck ordered the men back aboard. The *Maine* had received sailing orders for the next day, he explained. With the ship under orders, only officers could go ashore.

The orders sent the *Maine* to Norfolk, where the vessel was docked for more repairs. Lieutenant Commander Richard Wainwright replaced Lieutenant Commander Adolph Marix as executive officer; then, on December 11, 1897, the ship stood out of Hampton Roads for the last time, bound for Key West.

The *Maine* arrived there December 15, under orders to proceed to Havana any time United States Consul General Fitzhugh Lee asked for assistance.

Captain Sigsbee's first act at Key West was to arrange a code with the consul general in Havana, ninety miles south. He obtained the co-operation of an officer on the *Olivette*, a small American steamer that plied regularly between Key West and Havana. The officer would act as an intermediary, and the Spanish-controlled Havana post office would be by-passed. Through the agent on the *Olivette*, Lee and Sigsbee agreed that when Lee sent the words, "two dollars"—telegraphed or otherwise—the *Maine* would make preparations to start for Havana two hours after receiving another code.

The final message was to be, "Vessels might be employed elsewhere." On receipt of it, Sigsbee would get his ship under way for Havana without further notice.

"It was deemed necessary," Sigsbee recalled afterward, "to make occasional tests to ascertain if telegraphic communication continued open. Therefore, nearly every day I sent a message to General Lee, and he answered it.

"Some of these were rather absurd. In one I inquired of General Lee the state of the weather on the south side of Cuba. He promptly replied that he did not know— which was quite as gratifying as if he had been fully informed. At another time I cabled, 'What is the price of bullfight fans?' to which he replied, giving me quotations."

The *Maine* celebrated Christmas of '97 at Key West, but it was not exceedingly pleasant for the men.

"No extra dinners," Ambrose Ham noted in his log.

The ship did, however, mark the occasion by "illuminating" with hundreds of electric lights on Christmas Eve and again on Christmas night. The lights were strung fore and aft in a double rainbow across the mastheads and funnels, and a row of lights encircled the ship along the ridge rope of the awnings, at the height of the superstructure deck.

"One of the finest displays of electricity ever witnessed in the city," commented a local newspaper writer.

To most of the crew, unaware of the communications being exchanged by Sigsbee and Lee, the Key West visit seemed dull. Offering a bit of badly needed conversational material was a cold spell.

"One day we wore overcoats," Ham wrote, "and it is a strange thing to wear overcoats in Key West."

The liberty parties enjoyed little recreation ashore, aside from swimming on the beach after the cold snap had passed. But they did manage to attend baseball games. The men were proud of the ship's team and backed it vociferously in competition against other navy clubs.

Many officers and men were attending a game in the late afternoon of January 12, 1898, when Captain Sigsbee, on board the *Maine*, read a message from Consul General Lee. The words, "two dollars," caught Sigsbee's eye immediately.

A riot, evidently led by Spanish army officers who were followers of the ousted General Weyler, had broken out in Havana. Several newspaper offices had been attacked, but there was no evidence later of any intent to follow this up with attacks on Americans. It seemed to be a domestic fuss among Spanish factions. Still, Lee had become concerned enough to send the message.

At Key West, Sigsbee read the dispatch and at once gave orders for preparing the *Maine* for sea. He ordered a gun fired—a prearranged signal for all *Maine* men to return aboard—and the baseball game was called. Later, while awaiting the final message from Lee, Sigsbee and several of his officers went ashore to a dance, to divert the suspicion of correspondents. Several newspapers had stationed correspondents at Key West to report activities of the fleet and of principals in the Cuban trouble.

"I was asked a number of questions about the departure of the *Maine*," Sigsbee said later of this alert, "but we had managed so well that some of the crew had already given out that we were going to New York." The crew members did, in fact, believe that the *Maine* would head for New York upon departure from Key West.

The final message from Lee never arrived, and the *Maine* stayed at Key West for nearly two more weeks. During that time Sigsbee received orders to join the other ships of the North Atlantic Squadron when they arrived off Key West about January 23. All the ships, then, were to go to a fleet anchorage at nearby Dry Tortugas.

Sigsbee made plans for turning over the responsibility of keeping in contact with Consul General Lee to Lieutenant Albert Gleaves, commanding officer of the torpedo boat *Cushing,* which was to remain at Key West. He prepared a letter to Gleaves, telling him to report immediately if telegraphic service between Key West and Havana was disrupted, if he should at any time fail to get an answer from Lee, or if he should receive the code words, "pay nothing" (which had taken the place of the previously used "two dollars") or "vessels might be employed elsewhere."

The day after Sigsbee wrote his letter to Lieutenant Gleaves, the Secretary of the Navy wrote one—dated January 22—to Rear Admiral Sicard, squadron commander.

"The department directs you," the Secretary stated, "to order *Maine* and *Texas* to New Orleans by February 17 for Mardi Gras."

New Orleans citizens, in letters to the Secretary, had specifically requested that the *Maine* be instructed to make a return visit; the ship and its crew had made a hit the year before. But by February 17, and Mardi Gras time, the *Maine* was to be on the bottom of Havana Harbor.

Early Sunday morning, January 23, a *Maine* signalman sighted the other ships of the squadron and reported them to the officer of the deck. Several miles off Key West they anchored—the flagship *New York,* the *Iowa, Massachusetts, Indiana,* and *Texas.*

Immediately the *Maine,* accompanied by the *Montgomery* and *Detroit,* joined the squadron, and Sigsbee hurried over to the flagship to report to Admiral Sicard.

Later that day Captain French E. Chadwick, commanding officer of the *New York,* visited Sigsbee on board the *Maine.* Chadwick was aware of the probability of the *Maine*'s being ordered to Havana.

He later claimed to have said just before leaving the ship, "Look out, Sigsbee, that those fellows over there don't blow you up."

According to Chadwick, Sigsbee replied: "Don't worry. I've taken precautions enough against that."

That night the squadron remained at anchor close to Key West. Early next morning the ships weighed anchor for the Dry Tortugas, to the westward. As night was falling the squadron anchored there, but it was to be a short stay for the *Maine*.

The *New York* anchored in a position about six miles south of Tortugas, ordered the other ships to bank fires, and began sending night signals. Shortly before nine o'clock a quartermaster on the bridge of the *Maine* noticed, in the darkness to eastward, red and green rockets bursting in the sky. He notified the officer of the deck, who reported to the captain.

Sigsbee observed, through his binoculars, an approaching vessel. It was moving at a high speed, he realized, and he surmised that it was a dispatch boat, doubtless bringing orders from Key West for the *Maine*. Immediately he ordered fires spread and made other preparations for getting under way. He prepared to report aboard the flagship.

Sigsbee's guess soon proved to be accurate. The approaching vessel was the *Dupont*, carrying dispatches for Admiral Sicard. She made for the *New York*, arriving about thirty minutes after the *Maine* quartermaster had made his report. The *New York* signaled the *Maine* to prepare to get under way—Sigsbee replied immediately, "All ready"—and for the commanding officer to report aboard.

"I was in my gig and away almost before the signals had been answered," Sigsbee said.

Aboard the *New York*, he reported to Admiral Sicard, who had indeed received orders to send the *Maine* to Havana.

Sigsbee returned to his ship and instructed his officers to make the *Maine* ready for battle, but to do so without being obvious.

Frank Andrews, an ordinary seaman from Chemung, New York, who was to be killed in the explosion, described the night in a letter to his father.

"When orders were received to proceed to Havana," he said, "we saw that all our guns were in good order, cylinders filled, shot and shell out, and the decks almost cleared for action. Everything was ready for business, and we turned in for a couple of hours' sleep."

Captain Sigsbee, too, went to bed, after making a long entry in the night-order book when the *Maine* had weighed anchor about midnight. Sigsbee did not want to reach Havana at early daylight, preferring instead to steam into the harbor "when the town was alive and on its feet." He ordered a slow speed and a course that would bring a landfall well to the westward of the city.

Sigsbee went to bed unaware that General Lee had not asked for the *Maine*. Lee, in fact, wanted the visit postponed, but the State Department, obviously in a jittery mood, had plans of its own. Earlier that same day the department had telegraphed Lee:

"It is the purpose of this government to resume the friendly naval visits at Cuban ports. In that view, the *Maine* will call at the port of Havana in a day or two. Please arrange for a friendly interchange of calls with the authorities."

Lee had replied immediately, "Advise visit be postponed six or seven days to give last excitement time to disappear. Will see authorities, and let you know. Governor general away for two weeks. I should know day and hour visit."

Then, dutifully, Lee called on Spanish officials and reported the plans for the visit. The Spaniards, Lee advised the State Department, believed that the United States had an ulterior purpose in sending the ship, and they asked for a delay in its arrival until they could consult Madrid.

It was too late. The State Department wired back, but Lee did not receive the communication until the *Maine* had reached Havana:

"*Maine* has been ordered. Will probably arrive at Havana sometime tomorrow, Tuesday. Cannot tell hour. Possibly early. Co-operate with the authorities for her friendly visit. Keep us advised by frequent telegrams."

On board the *Maine*, most of the officers and crew not on watch were, like Frank Andrews and Captain Sigsbee, asleep. They had made all preparations, and whether the entry into Havana would indeed mean a "friendly visit" or a battle remained to be seen.

4

At Havana

The situation at Havana is still the same. In my opinion the arrival of the *Maine* causes the United States
government to dominate the situation.

—Captain Sigsbee, in
a letter to the Secretary of the Navy

Ambrose Ham stood a morning watch on January 25
when the *Maine* came within sight of the shores of Cuba.
He was signal boy of the watch; he had just traded duties
with another apprentice after Ham's division officer, Lieutenant Jungen, approved. The other apprentice wanted
to be in the crew of the captain's gig, where Ham had
been assigned, and the change of duty that he desired
was to cost him his life.

"As soon as it was daylight," Ham wrote in his log,
"we could see great hills of the island, almost hidden behind a morning mist. All the watch on deck were ordered

to clear away obstructions from the guns and to make the ship ready for fighting."

The *Maine*, however, was not actually cleared for action, as some American pacifists were to claim.

"That overshoots the mark," Captain Sigsbee commented later. "The *Maine* was merely in such a state of readiness that she could not have been taken at much disadvantage had she been attacked."

Frank Andrews added another paragraph to the letter to his father:

"We sighted Cuba at daylight, and all hands were soon on deck. We had heard that the Spaniards would fire on us, so we were prepared to return it with interest."

The *Maine* was about to be the first United States warship to visit Havana in three years. Three or four miles outside the harbor, boatswain's mates passed the word to man battle stations. Captain Sigsbee had made it clear that he did not want it to be obvious that the *Maine* was ready to fight, but he wanted his gun crews handy, and some men were even inside the turrets.

Gus Dressler stood inside the forward turret, and he could see absolutely nothing.

But Seaman First Class Michael J. Flynn of Philadelphia enjoyed a fine vantage point. He was on the forecastle, waiting to help with the mooring.

Flynn, twenty-two, a native of County Kildare, Ireland, had enlisted in the English navy when he was fifteen and served three years. In 1893 he had come to the United States, and in '94 he enlisted in the United States Navy. He discovered that it was a pleasant life after duty on the more strictly disciplined English ships.

Although Flynn had a fine vantage point, his interest was only casual. He already had seen more of the world than most of the crew. Besides, he was a professional sailor.

"I was the kind of a lad who didn't bother much," he said of the momentous entry of the *Maine* into Havana Harbor. "I just went along." Let the gold braid do the worrying, he thought to himself. He had another job to do: to get the *Maine* ready for mooring.

But Ambrose Ham was taking it all in with wide-eyed interest.

"As we entered the harbor everything looked peaceful," he said. His eyes were fixed on the "high rock" to the left of the entrance, atop which stood Morro Castle. The fort had been built by King Philip II during the period from 1589 to 1597, and about the only change since that time had been the addition of a lighthouse.

Most other sailors gazed at Morro too. From its height it seemed to dwarf the *Maine*. But Frank Andrews was not awed. He wrote:

"As we steamed in under the guns of Morro we calculated how long it would take us to silence it. Our turret-gun crews were standing out of sight, of course, while the rest of the crew was around the deck. At the first shot from the Spanish they would soon have found their places."

That shot, however, never came, and doubtless it had never occurred to the Spaniards to attempt it. The guns of Morro Castle continued to point over the *Maine* to seaward.

When, about 9:30 A.M., the *Maine* was close in to Morro, a harbor pilot, Julian Garcia Lopez, came aboard. Lopez showed Sigsbee a chart of the harbor and asked him if the vacant buoy number four would be a satisfactory berth. Sigsbee answered affirmatively; then he asked the Spanish pilot whether the *Maine* had been expected.

"No," Lopez answered. But Lopez stated in reply to another query that the *Maine* would be safe in Havana if the crew behaved, because Havana was "a cultured town."

Captain Sigsbee said later, "I could have taken the ship in myself, but I knew that the Spanish disliked the refusal of a pilot. I accepted one as an evidence of good will."

Lopez guided the ship in with professional skill. Nevertheless, Sigsbee and Lieutenant George F. W. Holman carefully observed the course changes.

As the *Maine* passed Morro Castle close to port, Ambrose Ham heard a sailor tell two friends: "We'll never get out of here alive." The two smiled and chided the sailor, and Ham thought that the man was embarrassed at making so grandiose a statement.

Then, to starboard, Ham observed the city of Havana, "almost level with the water." Somewhat behind the city was the harbor, and the Spanish pilot steered the ship to buoy number four, about four hundred yards off the Machina wharf, which was in the vicinity of the customhouse and the courthouse.

On the forecastle, Mike Flynn and the other men brought the last cruise of the *Maine* to a conclusion. At 10:00 A.M. they ran a chain through a ring on the buoy, brought the chain back aboard, and secured it.

Courtesies were now the concern of Captain Sigsbee, under orders to be particularly friendly. He had always made it a practice to observe strictly the required formalities, and he was well acquainted with them.

Upon the arrival of a foreign vessel in port, Sigsbee knew, the ship is expected to salute the flag of the nation to which the port belongs and to salute the senior naval officer present. He was also aware that the senior naval officer present would send an officer of the rank of lieutenant or below to the *Maine* with an offer of civilities. After the officer's departure, Sigsbee was to send a representative to the senior officer to acknowledge the visit and to express his thanks.

Then Sigsbee would be expected to call on all Spanish commanding officers of and above his rank. These visits would be returned within twenty-four hours.

Sigsbee also was to visit the highest civil and the highest military officer at the port and Consul General Lee.

Shortly after the *Maine* had been moored, a Spanish lieutenant came aboard, representing the senior naval officer present.

"His bearing was dignified and polite, the rule with Spanish naval officers," Sigsbee observed, "but I thought he looked embarrassed and even humiliated in carrying out his duty."

But Sigsbee was pleased to note that when another Spanish officer arrived the lieutenant seemed to lose his embarrassment.

Sigsbee was now ready to salute the Spanish flag and the admiral at Havana, but he wanted to be certain that both would be returned. He turned to the Spanish lieutenant and said, "I am about to give myself the honor of saluting your national flag. From which battery will the salute be returned?"

"From the Cabaña," answered the lieutenant.

Sigsbee ordered the two salutes fired, and both were returned—the one to the admiral by his flagship, *Alfonso XII.*

Sigsbee then made his official visits, and he was perfection itself. His calls were diplomatic and cordial.

"The Spanish officials on every hand gave us all the official courtesy to which we were entitled," Sigsbee said, "and they gave it with the grace of manner that is characteristic of their nation. I accepted it as genuine."

In full dress, including cocked hat, Sigsbee made his official visit to the Spanish admiral, Manterola. Landing at the Machina wharf, near the admiral's residence, he observed that a crowd had gathered. But there was no demonstration.

After the visit with Admiral Manterola, Sigsbee returned to the boat landing. He made it a point to observe the actions of the Spanish soldiers as he passed.

"They saluted me, as a rule," he said, "but with so much expression of apathy that the salute really went for nothing."

A few days later, Sigsbee had another chance to observe reactions of the people. Mazzantini, a celebrated Spanish bullfighter, was in Havana, and Sigsbee determined to attend one of the fights to observe again the feeling of the people of Havana toward the visit of the *Maine*. He informed General Parrado, acting captain general of the island in the absence of Ramon Blanco, of his desire to attend the bullfight, and Parrado immediately offered him tickets for a six-seat box. Sigsbee, Consul General Lee, and four *Maine* officers made up the party.

Shortly before they departed for the arena, Sigsbee and most of the other officers of the ship were entertained by Lee at a luncheon at the Havana Yacht Club several miles from the city. From there the six entrained for Havana.

En route, an American struck up a conversation with Sigsbee. Learning the captain's destination, the American advised him against going, explaining that "the common people on such occasions are generally excited." There was a probability, the man said, that a single cry against the naval officers might provoke an attack.

Sigsbee was not deterred. At the station, however, someone thrust a circular into his hand. Reports later stated
that a Spaniard was responsible, but Sigsbee said that he
thought the person was an American newspaper correspondent who wanted to inform him of the animosity in
some quarters.

The circular, in Spanish, contained a violent outburst
against Americans. Translated, it proclaimed:

Spaniards! . . . What are you doing that you allow your-
selves to be insulted in this way? Do you not see what they
have done to us in withdrawing our brave and beloved
Weyler, who at this very time would have finished with
this unworthy, rebellious rabble who are trampling on our
flag and on our honor?

Autonomy is imposed on us to cast us aside and give
places of honor and authority to those who initiated this
rebellion, these low-bred autonomists, ungrateful sons of
our beloved country.

And, finally, these Yankee pigs who meddle in our
affairs, humiliating us to the last degree, and, for a still
greater taunt, order to us a man-of-war of their rotten
squadron, after insulting us in their newspapers with articles sent from our own home.

Spaniards! The moment of action has arrived. Do not go
to sleep. Let us teach these vile traitors that we have not
yet lost our pride, and that we know how to protest with
the energy befitting a nation worthy and strong, as our
Spain is, and always will be!

Death to the Americans! Death to autonomy!

Long live Spain! Long live Weyler!

Sigsbee folded the circular, stuck it in a pocket, and
forgot it. He and Lee and the four officers took a ferry to
Regla, the site of the bullfight.

At the arena, Sigsbee discovered that his box was high

up, next to that of General Parrado. Sigsbee and his party took their seats, just as the first bull was being hauled away, and Parrado bowed. After that the general did not look in Sigsbee's direction again.

Four more bulls had been killed when General Lee suggested, in a low voice, that they leave "to avoid embarrassing General Parrado by mixing with the people."

They left then, just before the last bull entered the ring. Lee accompanied the officers back to the ship. About thirty minutes after their arrival, while Sigsbee and Lee were chatting on the quarter-deck, a ferry packed with people returning to Havana from the bullfight passed close to the *Maine*. The two men heard derisive calls and whistles. It was, however, the only demonstration made against the *Maine* during the entire visit.

Several days later, on February 11, the torpedo boat *Cushing* arrived with dispatches for the *Maine*, and the officers and crew discovered that misfortune had befallen a former shipmate.

Ensign J. C. Breckinridge, who previously had been a naval cadet on the *Maine*, had fallen overboard from the *Cushing* about an hour before, while that vessel was en route from Key West to Havana. John Everetts, a gunner's mate, had jumped into a rough sea to rescue Breckinridge, but when the officer was brought back aboard he was not breathing.

Crew members of the *Cushing* had taken turns at giving him artificial respiration, and when the ship reached Havana Harbor his body was rushed over to the *Maine*, where better medical facilities were available. Again artificial respiration was tried, but Breckinridge, as his former shipmates on the battleship realized, was dead.

The body lay in state on the poop deck of the *Maine* with a sailor standing watch over it. Later Chaplain Chidwick conducted a funeral service—three days before the explosion. Then Breckinridge's body was taken back aboard the *Cushing* and carried to Key West.

The crew members of the *Maine* regarded their stay in Havana with mixed emotions.

Ambrose Ham thought the visit was enjoyable enough. The days were perhaps too warm; but had the ship been around Norfolk, Boston, or New York, the weather would have been unpleasantly cold. Ham later remarked on the weather in his log:

"It was very warm at Havana. About 10:00 A.M. a breeze would spring up and last most of the day. At night, though, it would be calm and still."

The crew was allowed no liberty. Only officers in civilian clothes and men on official trips could go ashore. Ham did not mind this, although some of the other sailors grumbled. The food was fairly good, and this meant, to the young apprentice, happiness to a large degree.

But though Ham was generally satisfied in Havana, he found himself counting the months until his release from the navy.

"Time," he discovered, "was beginning to drag."

Ordinary Seaman Elmer Meilstrup of West Bay City, Michigan, was an extreme alarmist about the Havana visit. In a letter to his mother, Mrs. James S. Meilstrup (who received it two days after her son was reported missing), Elmer wrote:

"The Spaniards have a couple of gunboats and a cruiser, and there are two German gunboats. The guns of Morro Castle are pointed at us as I write. The whole bottom of the harbor is covered with torpedoes, so that if they did not want to let us out, we would not be able to go very well."

Two Newark, New Jersey, men had conflicting attitudes, expressed in letters to relatives (who also received the messages after the sailors' deaths).

Seaman Charles Dennig, like young Meilstrup, was an alarmist, and possibly a storyteller to boot. Despite the fact that the crew had no shore liberty in Havana, he wrote a relative:

"A crowd of us went ashore one day to enjoy ourselves, and when we got into Havana a crowd of Spaniards gathered around us and tried to kill us, but we licked a couple of them and fought our way out."

Coal Passer Thomas Clark, however, wrote his father in a different tone.

"It was current that our ship received an order to leave within 24 hours or there would be trouble, but as to the exact truth I cannot say. I feel as safe on board the *Maine* as I would in Newark."

Still another letter-writing sailor, Seaman Andrew Erikson of Union Hill, New Jersey, penned a description of the stay in Havana Harbor; his letter was received by a friend just before the explosion.

"You wrote about our going to New Orleans," said Erikson, referring to the fact that the *Maine* had been ordered to the Louisiana city to participate in the Mardi Gras festival. "Don't you believe anything of the kind. We will probably stay here a couple of months, for there is liable to be trouble at any time. We are standing watches every night and are keeping a good lookout for any small boat, for you can't tell what kind of mischief the Spaniards are up to."

Watch-standers aboard the *Maine* had indeed been instructed to keep a sharp lookout. And Captain Sigsbee had ordered a quarter watch at night, instead of the usual in-port anchor watch, so that one fourth of the crew was instantly available to man secondary-battery guns forward and aft.

The captain also instructed Lieutenant Commander Wainwright to see to it that a supply of six-inch ammunition was kept on hand. Sentries, also supplied with ammunition, paced the forecastle and poop deck at night, and the marine corporal of the guard, the officer of the deck, and a quartermaster guarded the two gangways.

"I personally instructed the master-at-arms and the orderly sergeant to keep a careful eye on every visitor who came on board," Captain Sigsbee said. "I instructed them to follow visitors about at a proper distance whenever the ship was visited below. They were to watch for any packages that might be laid down or left by these people."

Sigsbee also ordered the dipping lines of the collision mats "rove and kept standing."

Having ordered as many precautionary measures as possible without making an outward show of animosity, Sigsbee seemed confident that the *Maine* was safe. He felt certain enough to write the new Secretary of the Navy, John D. Long, to that effect early in February. In that letter he added a suggestion that the *Maine*, when relieved, should not be replaced by a smaller vessel, but by the *Texas, Massachusetts,* or *Indiana.*

Two days later Sigsbee followed up with a letter containing suggestions for commanding officers of ships ordered to Havana in the future. He advised against using harbor water even to wash down the decks, explaining that it "has a foul smell when stirred up by passing vessels." Sigsbee also suggested provisioning in Key West, because food was expensive in Havana.

While Captain Sigsbee busied himself with these letters,

Apprentice Ham was interested in observing a strange custom followed in the Spanish fleet.

"While we were there," he wrote, "we watched the Spaniards every evening at sundown run up the masts and chase the devils out of the gear blocks.

"Some years ago a Spanish sailing ship got into a gale and when they tried to take in sail the blocks would not work. The ship capsized."

During the entire visit the officers and crew of the *Maine* never slackened their vigilance. Until the night of the explosion, however, no one had any indication that precautions were actually necessary.

5

The Last Day

The atmosphere was heavy; the easterly trade wind
had fallen flat. Occasionally I heard the sound of a
passing ferry boat. Otherwise the harbor was very
quiet.

—Captain Sigsbee, in
Century magazine

Ambrose Ham lay sleeping in the third compartment
from the bow on the port side of the berth deck. From
hammocks near his came the varied snores of a dozen or
more crewmen of the *Maine*.

A boatswain's mate entered the compartment and
looked from one man to another. He seemed to relish
the thought of what he was about to do.

"Reveille," he croaked in a gravelly voice.

Ham, wishing for a few more minutes in his hammock,
forced his eyes open. A glance at the boatswain's mate
told him he had better get out of the hammock without
delay, and his bare feet hit the deck with a slap. Five-

thirty was, Ham thought, an ungodly hour for arising. This was to be the day for the *Maine* to make history, but the routine remained unchanged. Ham rubbed his eyes, lashed up his hammock, and went to the galley for coffee to purge himself of his sleepiness. After a gulp of the steaming liquid he lost his drowsiness, but droplets of perspiration dotted his forehead; the coffee compounded the perpetual sultriness of Havana. On a morning like this Ham occasionally found himself wishing briefly for the bone-chilling February he had been used to on the farm in New York.

From reveille until 7:30 Ham and the other crew members turned to at cleaning the ship. They washed down the decks with fresh water from a lighter that came alongside—the medical officer, confirming Captain Sigsbee's judgment, had banned the use of the contaminated harbor water—and they polished bright work.

At 7:30 A.M. the crew was piped to breakfast, and Ham, having worked up an appetite for two hours, ate the oatmeal and drank more coffee ravenously—and quickly, for he was to have the 8:00–12:00 A.M. watch and had to relieve the poop-deck signalman so he could have breakfast too.

In Havana Harbor at this time Ham had little to do on watch. As signal boy his primary duty was to handle wigwag messages between naval vessels, but no other United States Navy ships had been in the harbor since the U.S.S. *Cushing* departed three days earlier.

Ham had been ordered, however, to keep a sharp lookout for any suspicious movement in the vicinity of the *Maine*, and he occupied his time during the forenoon watch scrutinizing the ship and the area around it.

Looking down on the main deck from the poop, he saw the crew mustered, as usual, for 9:30 A.M. quarters. The men were inspected by their officers. Next Ham noticed that the ship was swinging. It swung, he observed, so that its bow pointed toward the city.

Ham saw, however, absolutely nothing of what he had been ordered to watch for: suspicious movement. Promptly at noon he was relieved by another apprentice, and he hurried down to dinner.

Late that afternoon, after ship's work had halted for the day, Ham did some sewing. He was getting to be quite a hand at this since a shipmate had taught him the fundamentals of the handiwork.

"At five o'clock," he wrote, "quarters were sounded, and we had a little setting-up drill."

At 5:30 P.M. the marine bugler, C. H. Newton of Washington, D.C., sounded the call to supper. At 6:00 P.M. Ham and his shipmates turned to at sweeping down decks, but this required only fifteen minutes or so. After that all the chores for another day aboard the *Maine* were done. The rest of the time, with the exception of night watches, was free. Ham, listed also for the 8:00–12:00 P.M. signal watch on the poop, spent most of an hour listening to a shipmate play an accordion while some of the sailors danced to the rollicking music.

A few feet from the group stood Naval Cadet Cluverius, who, nearly two years earlier, had put Ham on report for slowness in obeying orders. Cluverius had the 4:00– 8:00 quarter-deck watch. "Nothing of event" had occurred, and now—about 7:30 P.M.—he was looking forward to being relieved.

The young cadet listened to the accordion music and watched the sailors dance. He heard, coming from the after turret, the sound of a mandolin. A gunner's mate there was entertaining a smaller audience.

Bugler Newton, from his position aft on the main deck,

interrupted the gaiety with the call for hammocks. Ham pushed himself up from the deck where he had been sitting. He went below, slung his hammock, and made it ready. When he came off watch at midnight he could turn in without delay.

Several other members of the crew, after slinging their hammocks, returned to the main deck for more music and dancing, but it was time for Ham to relieve the watch. At eight o'clock he ascended the ladder to the poop deck.

At that same moment, Cluverius was being relieved as officer of the deck by Lieutenant John J. Blandin. Before turning over the deck, however, he had taken the eight o'clock reports and had heard the various duty petty officers report the ship secure for the night.

Cluverius went to his quarters and discovered that this was almost like walking into an oven. He stripped to his underclothing and began getting his letters ready for posting tomorrow. The *Olivette*, he knew, was scheduled to enter port in the morning and to depart a few hours later for Key West with mail from the *Maine*.

On deck, the music to which Cluverius and Ham had been listening continued until Newton sounded first call.

From a stuffy stateroom in the after part of the ship, just below the deck where Ambrose Ham was standing his watch, Captain Sigsbee could hear the frolicking.

For the sake of comfort Sigsbee had taken off his blouse and put on a thin civilian jacket. He was writing, completing a report to Theodore Roosevelt, Assistant Secretary of the Navy, "on the advisability of continuing to place torpedo tubes on board cruisers and battleships." Sigsbee opposed the practice.

Actually, Sigsbee was not at this time in his own quarters. The *Maine* had been fitted out as a flagship; an admiral's stateroom, never occupied, adjoined the captain's cabin. The two cabins were symmetrical in arrangement, the captain's being on the starboard side and the admiral's to port. A door connected the two cabins, so Sigsbee used both. Now he sat at a table in the admiral's quarters, working on the report to Mr. Roosevelt.

Sigsbee had begun working on the report about 8:00 P.M. He had been unable to give it his attention during the afternoon; several visitors had taken up his time. Shortly after nine o'clock he completed it and began a letter to his wife. This soon proved to be an unpleasant task. For in a pocket of the thin jacket, which he was wearing for the first time aboard the *Maine*, the captain discovered a letter to his wife that he had neglected to give her months earlier. He was struggling to apologize when, at 9:10 P.M., taps sounded.

"I laid down my pen to listen to the notes of the bugle, which were singularly beautiful in the oppressive stillness of the night. The bugler, Newton, who was given to fanciful effects, was evidently doing his best. During his pauses the echoes floated back with distinctness, repeating the strains fully and exactly."

Then the echo of the last note faded away, and Sigsbee again took up his pen. The letter required a great deal of thought, he had discovered, and he could not write it hurriedly.

While Sigsbee wrote, Seaman Flynn, the English navy veteran, crawled into his hammock in the forecastle, said his prayers like a good Catholic, and fell asleep almost immediately.

Above, on the main deck, Lieutenant Blandin, officer of the deck, peered down the darkened hatches to see that everything was secure. Then he walked to the rail and looked over the starboard side.

Blandin had learned to be cautious by experience. He had been aboard the *Trenton* at Samoa in March, 1889, when a storm wrecked five American and German warships and claimed the lives of 244 men.

After Blandin had made his brief security check and found "everything normal," he walked aft of the quarterdeck, behind the rear turret, as the watch officer was allowed to do after eight o'clock in the evening. There, on the port side of the ship, he sat for a few minutes in quiet reflection. His disinterested gaze rested on the murky harbor water. Ahead, off the port bow, the lights of Havana seemed to be winking at him.

The ship, Blandin had observed when he came on watch, had swung so that its bow pointed toward the city. It lay in a position that it would have assumed had the starboard batteries been brought to bear on Spanish fortifications protecting the harbor entrance and the port batteries on defense works protecting the land side of the city. Usually it did not lie this way; the prevailing easterly breeze caused the ship to face into the wind.

Blandin felt a bit glum. He had hoped for orders to other duty before now, but they had not arrived. The dark, overcast sky, which threatened rain, seemed to reflect his mood.

After a few minutes Blandin arose, walked to the starboard side, and again seated himself in silent reflection.

"I was so quiet that Lieutenant [John] Hood came up and asked laughingly if I was asleep," Blandin recalled later. "I said, 'No, I am on watch.'"

The time was a few seconds before 9:40 P.M., and Blandin hoped that the next two hours and twenty minutes would move more swiftly than the first part of the watch.

Below deck, Marine First Lieutenant A. W. Catlin had,

like Captain Sigsbee, retired to his room to write a letter. Earlier he had received mail from his cousin, George Catlin of Paterson, New Jersey, and he was determined to answer it.

Catlin discovered that his room was much too warm for comfort. He stripped off his coat, required to be worn outside his quarters, and hung it up. Then, seated at his desk, he lighted a Cuban cigar and serenely blew out a cloud of smoke.

"The thought passed through my mind," he wrote his cousin later, "how much you would enjoy one of the superb Havanas on such a night. The water and the sky were so peaceful, so calm, that the very air held a certain stillness unfelt in northern waters."

Catlin had mislaid his pen. He looked under a pile of papers and leisurely browsed through other items on his desk, but he was unable to locate it. He blew another cloud of smoke. The letter could wait a while longer.

On the poop deck, Ambrose Ham talked with a friend for a few minutes after taps sounded and the music and dancing stopped. Then his friend, fearful of being caught on deck after taps, turned in, and Ham was left with his thoughts. The night could scarcely be quieter, he realized, and the water was as smooth as a lake. Several hundred yards away he could see one or two small boats, but none came near enough to require him to make a report to the officer of the deck.

The night was warm—like a July night in New York, he thought to himself. His recollection of New York led to memories of home, and, although he rarely became homesick, Ham found himself longing for the day when he would be discharged from the navy and would be on his own. He certainly would return to New York State, he decided.

The night watches, Ham reflected, were bad for a man's morale. They allowed entirely too much time for meditation, and the time passed too slowly. It was better for a man to be busy.

Then Ham remembered that a friend—Quartermaster Third Class Millard F. Harris of Boothbay Harbor, Maine —was on the bridge. Ham and Harris "chummed together," and on a night like this, in port, they co-operated in brewing coffee. About halfway through a watch one of them—Ham one night and Harris the next—would take a stewpan "appropriated from the galley," find some coffee ("if we couldn't get it from our own mess we'd get it from another one"), and go below to the engine room. There an obliging fireman would retrieve a shovelful of hot coals, and Ham or his friend would add water to the coffee and put the stewpan on the coals to boil.

This Tuesday night it was Ham's turn to make the coffee. About 9:30, becoming weary of the slow-moving watch, he contacted his friend on the bridge and asked whether he was ready.

"Well," Harris said, "it's a little early yet. Better wait awhile."

So for a few more minutes Ham leaned listlessly on the railing, thought about Schenectady, and wished for midnight.

In the port gangway, Marine Corporal Frank G. Thompson of Charlestown, Massachusetts, had made himself snug in his hammock. He had no watches scheduled and was looking forward to enjoying an uninterrupted sleep. He had read a book until taps, when he had carried it down to the mail orderly, Sergeant James T. Brown, in the master-at-arms compartment. Then Thompson had visited the head and, about 9:25, had returned to his hammock.

While Thompson rested comfortably under a thin blanket, Master-at-Arms Third Class John B. Load, an Englishman, talked with the duty M.A., Charles Laird of Everett, Massachusetts. Laird told him where to find the keys to the brig and other compartments if Load should need them during the night. Then Load went to his hammock, slung outside the armory door underneath the middle superstructure. He took off his shirt and tossed it on the hammock. He looked over at Landsman William Caulfield of New Orleans, Louisiana, and envied his sleep.

Far below the deck where Load stood, almost at the bottom of the ship, Fireman First Class William Gartrell of Washington, D.C., lay down on a mattress in the steam-steering engine room with a book he intended to read.

Gartrell had charge of the engineers' storeroom. Only minutes before, Chief Machinist William Rushworth of Norfolk, Virginia, had asked for and obtained from him the storeroom keys. Gartrell had requested the chief to leave them near his shoes when he was finished with them.

Then Gartrell picked up the book, but Oiler Charles F. Quinn of Boston, on watch, interrupted him again.

"We want some oil," Quinn said.

Gartrell rose and handed him another set of keys. Quinn unlocked a door, got the oil he needed, and tossed the keys back to Gartrell, who by now had given up the idea of reading. Instead, he flopped down on his mattress, beside Coal Passer Frank Gardner of New York City, and closed his eyes.

But Gardner wanted to talk. The two men began comparing the amount of time left on their respective enlistments. Gardner said he was due for discharge in May; Gartrell replied that his time would be up in June. Gardner answered jokingly that he would stay on and wait for him.

Elsewhere on the ship, other crewmen and officers had by this time begun to enjoy relaxing from the day's work. Some occupied themselves with personal business. Many were asleep.

Chaplain Chidwick had retired to his quarters, where he read the office of the day. Finishing it, he reached for a book, *Facts and Fakes About Cuba*, by George Bronson Rea.

But Alonzo Willis, an apprentice from Keyport, New Jersey, was standing a quarter watch on the poop, near Ambrose Ham. Willis anticipated some sleep soon. He was to be relieved at ten o'clock instead of midnight.

Another man on watch, Gus Dressler, chatted with a friend near a six-pounder gun. Dressler had just been sent by the bridge quartermaster to make a report to the officer of the deck on the quarter-deck, and he was in no hurry to return to his watch station.

One hundred yards from the *Maine*, two passengers on the American steamer *City of Washington* also were chatting as they studied the silhouette of the darkened American warship from the stern of their vessel. They were Sigmond Rothschild of Detroit, a tobacco packer in Cuba since 1871, and Louis Wertheimer of New York City, a dealer in leaf tobacco.

Both men had been relaxing in the smoking room of the ship until shortly after 9:30 P.M., when Rothschild suggested they go to the stern and look at the *Maine*.

Rothschild had joked about it when the two men reached the deck chairs there.

"We're well protected here," he said, "under the guns of the United States."

They observed that all was quiet on the *Maine*. The music they had heard coming from the warship while the *City of Washington* had been entering the harbor an hour or so earlier had stopped. Not even many lights were visible on the *Maine* now.

Ashore, Frank Weinheimer, another New Yorker visiting Cuba, studied the outline of the warship from a wharf, where he and many other persons had strolled to catch what little breeze the night offered. Shortly before 9:40 P.M. he noticed the forms of several topside watch-standers. They were pacing to and fro.

6

The Explosion

I was in the gangway when I first heard this explosion.
The next thing I knew about it I was fired overboard
in the water—lifted clean off the gangway and fired
in the water.

—Sergeant Michael Meehan,
U.S. Marine Corps

Captain Sigsbee signed his name to the letter and addressed an envelope to his wife with a feeling of relief. He
laid down his pen, folded the letter, picked up the envelope. He was enclosing the letter in the envelope when
he heard a terrible noise.

To Sigsbee it was "a bursting, rending, crashing roar
of immense volume." He felt the ship tremble and list to
port.

On the poop deck above, Ambrose Ham, after exchang-
ing a few words with Landsman Thomas J. Waters of
Philadelphia, had been about to turn around and walk aft
when he saw a flame shoot up and envelop the whole for-

ward part of the ship. He heard a roar, and almost immediately he was struck by a heavy object. For a few seconds he was senseless.

On the stern of the *City of Washington*, Sigmond Rothschild and Louis Wertheimer had reached for their two
deck chairs to carry them closer to the rail where they
could rest their feet, when they heard a noise. Rothschild
thought it was like "a shot." Wertheimer called it "a report, a minor report."

"I looked around and saw the bow of the *Maine* rise a little, go a little out of the water," Rothschild said. "It
couldn't have been more than a few seconds after that
noise that there came in the center of the ship a terrible
mass of fire and explosion, and everything went over our
heads."

At the gangway of the *City of Washington*, First Officer
George Cornell had been giving the quartermaster orders
for calling the men at five o'clock in the morning when he
heard "a rumbling sound," looked up, and saw the *Maine*
rise up at the bow. Before he had time to think, he was
shaken by the concussion of a giant explosion.

Near Cornell, in a cabin on the *City of Washington*,
José M. Mann of New York City had been conversing with
other passengers when a loud report startled them. They
rushed to the portholes in time to see a sheet of flame
erupt from the forward part of the *Maine*. This was accompanied by another—and much greater—explosion.
The awed witnesses saw debris and several bodies tossed
into the air. Cries for help reached their ears. Their first
thought was that shore batteries had fired on the *Maine*.
When they heard wreckage from the battleship striking
the exterior of their own vessel, they mistook it to mean
that the *City of Washington* also was under attack.

On a nearby wharf, Frank Weinheimer, the New

Yorker who had been observing the silhouette of the
Maine, heard a crunching sound, "like the breaking of
crockery." Then he, too, was startled by a terrific roar.

"To me," he said, "it looked as if the whole inside of
the ship had blown out."

Several persons near Weinheimer were almost thrown
off their feet by the force of the explosion. The air around
him became hot and thick with smoke, and nearly everyone, he said, grew panicky.

On the *Maine*, the only men not instantly aware of the
explosion were those killed outright, and there were more
than 250 of them. The explosion came from the forward
part of the ship—and somewhat to port—where most of
the crew slept. The officers, quartered aft, were more fortunate. The force of the explosion devastated the forward
part of the *Maine* and even curled it back upon itself.

Naval Cadet Cluverius had been writing in his room
when "a report—the firing of a gun, it seemed," startled
him. This was followed by "an indescribable roar, a terrific crash, and intense darkness." The deck beneath him
seemed to give way.

He felt his way to the messroom and bumped into Naval
Cadet Amon Bronson, Jr.

"Come on," Bronson urged. "We'll make it."

In the passageway they discovered that water was already ankle-deep. They felt a draft of air from forward
and realized that the sides or the main deck of the ship
must have been blown away.

When the two cadets reached the junior officers' hatch
they found it blocked by wreckage. They turned aft then
and passed the engine-room hatch, down which water was
pouring on the men trapped below. The cadets struggled
up the ladder of the wardroom hatch and out through a
passageway.

On the quarter-deck, where he had been standing his watch, Lieutenant Blandin heard a "dull, sullen" roar. Still near him then was Lieutenant Hood. Immediately after the roar, Blandin heard a sharp explosion. "A perfect train of missiles of all description, from huge pieces of cement to blocks of wood, steel railings, and fragments of gratings" rained down on them. A piece of cement struck Blandin on the head and sent him sprawling, but he quickly scrambled to his feet.

Hood, horrified to see the entire deck forward thrown into the air, had leaped for cover and then run aft. A flying object knocked off his cap as he ran. Miraculously, it did not strike him, but he felt the wind created by its passage.

Blandin started after Hood.

"I supposed that Hood was dazed by the shock and about to jump overboard," Blandin said later. "I hailed him, and he answered that he was running to the poop to help lower the boats."

From the forward section that had blown up, Seaman Mike Flynn had somehow escaped with his life. The explosion blew him upward—the deck above him must have opened up first—and he remembered later that he actually seemed to be dreaming about flying through the air.

Flynn was unconscious for several seconds until the cool, filthy harbor water revived him, and he then thought that he was about to drown. He struggled to the surface amidst burning wreckage, instantly dived under again, and began swimming away from the vicinity of the ship. But swimming was painful. He later discovered, after he had been picked up by a boat from the Spanish cruiser *Alfonso XII*, that his left hip and left shoulder were dislocated.

The explosion had blown many other men into the water. Ordinary Seaman John Heffron of Brooklyn was hurtled through the air with the forward ten-inch turret, and he said later that he never knew which of the two landed in the harbor first.

Landsman Michael Lanahan of Louisville, Kentucky, was thrown from his forecastle hammock into water fifty yards to starboard. He swam to a nearby buoy and discovered that his only injury was a slight head cut.

Apprentice Alonzo Willis, the Keyport, New Jersey, sailor, was blown from his watch area near the stern into water several yards away from the ship.

Ordinary Seaman William Mattisen of West Bay City, Michigan, however, stayed on the ship. He was standing messenger watch in the starboard gangway when the explosion tossed him nearly straight up. He landed on his shoulder several feet aft of the spot he had occupied.

Apprentice Gus Dressler also stayed on the ship. He was hurled into space, knocked senseless, and left sitting on a hammock netting two or three feet away from the vicinity of the six-pounder, where he had been conversing with his friend. When Dressler regained consciousness several minutes later he realized that his feet were dangling in the harbor water. Still later, he learned that his injuries included burns, a broken jaw, and a dislocated knee.

Landsman George Fox of Manitowoc, Wisconsin, was thrown out of his bunk in the lamp room; somehow, he landed feet first. He could see nothing, but an overpowering smell of powder almost gagged him, and he heard men groaning nearby. After he finally found an opening and crawled through it he realized that the lamp room was almost upside down.

The force of the explosion capsized a steam launch tied

up at the starboard boom, and the boat carried five occupants far underwater before they were able to free themselves.

In the boat were Coxswain Benjamin R. Wilbur of Philadelphia; Fireman First Class John H. Panck of Lynchburg, Virginia; Coal Passer Charles A. Lohman of Sweden; Seaman Peter Mikkelsen of Denmark; and Seaman Arthur Rau, a native German. Miraculously, all five survived.

Wilbur came up close to what he took to be a coaling boom and saw Panck already on it. Rau, meanwhile, had encountered great difficulty reaching the surface, striking underwater objects three times before he finally managed to get to the top. Nearby he saw Mikkelsen, and the two men shouted for help. After several minutes they were picked up by a Spanish shore boat.

Wilbur stayed for a while on the coaling boom; then he reflected on the possibility of sharks and quickly swam back to the ship. He struggled aboard at the starboard gangway, appalled at the extent of destruction.

Far below deck, Fireman Gartrell frantically felt for a ladder on the port side of the engine room. He had no sooner heard Coal Passer Gardner vow jokingly to stay on past his discharge date than "a blue flash," apparently coming from the steering engine room, startled both of them.

A roar followed the flash, and they jumped from their mattresses. In the darkness that now enveloped the engine room, Gartrell ran for the port ladder. Gardner made for one on the starboard side. Evidently he struck his head on a metal object. Dazed and helpless, he called to Gartrell:

"Billy, I'm gone!"

Gartrell, in water up to his knees and aware that the ship was sinking rapidly, did not stop. He found the port ladder and hurried up to the compartment above. There he became confused. The room was so dark he could see nothing, and he stumbled over several objects in his frantic efforts to find another ladder leading upward.

Meanwhile, Marine Lieutenant Catlin, looking for his fountain pen when the ship blew up, had rushed out of his darkened room in shirt sleeves. He groped his way to a hatch and reached the main deck uninjured.

Another marine, however, lay stunned in the port gangway. Corporal Frank G. Thompson had been lying awake in his hammock, looking forward to enjoying an uninterrupted sleep, when he was abruptly tossed into the air and through an awning that covered the deck. Then he hit the awning again and struck the deck on his side. When he recovered his senses—he was blown so high he had had a view of the superstructure—the thought entered his mind that war had started and that the Spaniards had opened fire. He heard men groaning and crying for help, and he realized that the ship was sinking.

Somewhere below the main deck, Master-at-Arms Load also was aware that the *Maine* was going down. An explosion had sent him sprawling—perhaps he was thrown into the air first—and when he recovered his senses he realized that he must have tumbled through a hatch. He was below the main deck and water was flooding the compartment.

Near him he recognized the excited voices of Gunner's Mate Third Class James Williams, who had been sleeping near Load, Landsman Joseph H. Kane, and Marine Private William McGuinness. The three of them, like Load, were pinned by wreckage.

At first Load believed that a boiler had exploded; the water seemed hot to him, and he was choked by smoke. He thought he would suffocate. He and the others were coughing violently. For relief they drank the dirty harbor water as it rose around them.

Load told Kane he had given up all hope. Kane had replied with a similar admission when still another, but less severe, explosion jarred them. This one shook them free of the debris. The four men managed to crawl up on wreckage piled in the compartment and squeeze through an opening to the port side of the upper superstructure.

The port awning, Load observed, was aflame, and several injured men were lying helpless on it. One of them, Ship's Cook First Class George Schwartz of Germany, shouted Load's name. Load threw him the end of a piece of wire rope and pulled him off. Then Load helped off Marine Privates Joseph Lutz and C. P. Galpin, and two or three others whose names he did not know.

While Load was trying frantically to save the lives of several mates, four officers were striving to reach the main deck from the wardroom.

In the after part of the messroom Lieutenants Holman, Jungen, and Jenkins had been engaged in an intense conversation—Chief Engineer Charles P. Howell had been sitting, uninvolved, nearby—when the explosion occurred and the lights went out.

"We've been torpedoed!" Holman shouted. "Get up on deck."

Jungen stated later that Holman called out, "Follow me," but Holman himself said that in the darkness he could not see whether the others were ahead of or behind him. Probably, however, he was in front, with Jungen and Jenkins following in that order.

Holman felt his way to the wardroom ladder leading to

the main deck and scurried up it. Jungen stretched out his arms and found his way to the ladder too.

"I knew where I was, but I was afraid of missing my way," Jungen said.

Chief Engineer Howell also hauled himself up the ladder. Jenkins, however, lost his way, stumbling about helplessly in the messroom in water now up to his waist.

Mess Attendant John H. Turpin encountered Jenkins there. Turpin had been sitting near the icebox in the wardroom pantry, talking with Mess Attendants Westmore Harris and Robert White, when the ship blew up. Immediately Turpin had headed topside too, but he had blundered into the messroom. Now he heard Lieutenant Jenkins' voice.

"Which way?" Jenkins asked.

"I don't know which way," Turpin answered.

"Which way?" Jenkins shouted.

"I don't know, sir, which way."

But Jenkins asked a third time.

"Which way?"

"I don't know, sir."

Turpin groped his way aft through chest-deep water toward where he thought a ladder might be. Jenkins started forward.

"Then the whole compartment lit right up," Turpin recalled. "The whole compartment where the torpedoes were lit right up, and I saw Mr. Jenkins throw up both hands and fall, right by the steerage pantry."

Water had reached Turpin's chin. He struggled as quickly as possible to the ladder, but when he arrived at the spot where it should have been he found nothing. The ladder, of wood, probably had floated away.

Turpin felt a rope touch his arm, and he pulled himself up to the main deck. From there he ascended the ladder to the poop deck and encountered Lieutenant Holman, who was still under the impression that the *Maine* had been attacked by Spanish forces.

"Go below and get some cutlasses," Holman told him.

"Aye, aye, sir," answered the obedient but reluctant mess attendant.

Turpin went below to the after gun room. He found the water rising so swiftly that he came up again and jumped overboard. He began swimming away from the ship.

John Herbert, the whaleboat crewman who had used his belt and an oar to fashion a rudder during the Hatteras storm, grabbed his ankle.

"Let go, please," Turpin implored. "You'll drown the two of us."

Herbert would not let go. Instead, he climbed on Turpin's back. Turpin hit him, and Herbert relinquished his hold. Both men were rescued later, but not until Turpin had observed a Spanish boat nearby and, thinking it was an enemy, dived under the water.

Almost directly below the deck where Turpin had dived overboard from the *Maine*, Fireman Gartrell realized that someone had joined him in the flooded compartment from which he was still seeking escape. The man was Mess Attendant Westmore Harris, with whom Turpin had been talking when the ship exploded. Harris had lost his sense of direction and, instead of finding the main deck, had wandered about below.

"There's no hope," Gartrell said to the man. Then Gartrell began praying, a thing he had rarely done. But soon he heard, a few yards away, the sound of someone's voice. Looking around, he saw a faint light. He and Harris struggled toward it. When they drew closer they found an opening and squirmed through. On the main deck Gartrell tried to say another prayer, but fainted.

Coal Passer Thomas Melville of New York City came upon the slumped form of Gartrell. Melville, with Seamen Harry McCann and Peder Larsen, had been on the quarter-deck, on the port side near the after turret, when the explosion rocked the *Maine*.

Larsen was thrown to the poop deck. Melville, still on the quarter-deck, wiped ashes off his face and out of his eyes and saw the steam launch at the starboard boom capsize under a hail of debris.

Observing that Larsen was not around, Melville and McCann started off after a few minutes in the direction of the starboard gangway. Coxswain Wilbur, who by now had swum back to the ship from the coaling boom, joined them as they came upon Gartrell.

Then Melville noticed the lifeless body of Boatswain's Mate Second Class Luther Lancaster lying nearby. He saw another man he did not know clinging in the water to the gangway. Melville stooped to pull him aboard and, noticing that he was not breathing, left the body sprawled on deck.

Several yards away, Captain Sigsbee calmly gave orders to save as many lives as possible, but he had not yet realized the scope of the disaster.

After Sigsbee had heard the roar of the explosion, the eight electric lights in the cabin had gone out almost immediately, and he was left groping in "intense blackness and smoke."

With the ship listing to port, Sigsbee had walked up an inclined deck to the starboard side, and for a moment he had thought only of saving himself. His eye fell on the starboard ports, faintly relieved against the background of the overcast sky. The sashes were out of them, and the openings were large. His first intention had been to escape through one of the ports.

Then, however, the habit of command returned, and he chose a more dignified way of making an exit: along the passageway leading forward through the superstructure.

While he was feeling his way out to the main deck a marine private bumped into him. It was William Anthony, the captain's orderly; he mumbled his apologies and reported that the ship was sinking. Sigsbee told the man to return to the quarter-deck and followed him.

There Sigsbee stood for a moment on the starboard side and tried to take in the situation, but he could see nothing distinctly. He asked Anthony for the exact time.

"The explosion took place at 9:40, sir," replied the marine.

Sigsbee realized that the *Maine* was settling rapidly. He and several of his officers retreated to the poop deck, a few feet higher. Most of the other officers and surviving enlisted men had gathered there, including the executive officer, Lieutenant Commander Wainwright.

Wainwright had been standing in the captain's office, talking with Naval Cadet Jonas Holden, when the ship blew up. They heard the falling wreckage and presumed that the Spaniards were firing at the *Maine*.

Wainwright and Holden had rushed out on deck, gaped at the flaming forward part of the ship, and headed for the poop deck. There the executive officer soon recognized the captain's voice giving orders.

"As near as I can recollect," Wainwright said later, "the captain told me to see that the boats were lowered. I gave the order to clear them away."

Only three of the fifteen boats had been left serviceable, but Wainwright discovered that there were few enlisted men around to help lower even these. He moved from davit to davit, seeing that people were standing by to put the boats in the water. Most of the helpers were officers.

One of them was Naval Cadet D. F. Boyd, Jr. Boyd had been in the junior officers' messroom, reading, when he heard the crash and saw the lights go out. He was struck on the back of the head by a piece of wood and knocked unconscious. When he recovered he felt someone nearby; it proved to be Assistant Engineer Darwin Merritt of Red Oaks, Iowa.

Grasping Merritt's hand, Boyd insisted they hurry topside. Merritt, however, was dazed. Boyd pulled him into the passage in the after torpedo room.

"We groped along the bulkhead until we came to the turn going over to the port side," Boyd said. "At this moment the ship sank down amidships and heeled over to port, and the rush of water swept us apart."

Merritt, a former Annapolis halfback, drowned, but Boyd clung to a steam pipe above, keeping his head out of the rising water. He made his way hand over hand along the pipe to the spot where a ladder should have been. It was gone.

By this time the water, rushing through the ports, was almost over Boyd's head. At that instant, however, some burning cellulose flared up on deck, and Boyd saw a hatch. He escaped through it after climbing over a pile of wreckage.

On the poop deck, Boyd helped lower the boats; then he heard Captain Sigsbee tell Wainwright to flood the magazines. The executive officer answered, "There's no use flooding the magazines, Captain; the ship is sinking."

Wainwright then called for volunteers to go forward with him to try to extinguish the fire. Boyd and Lieutenant Hood offered their services.

Climbing over wreckage, the three made their way far enough forward to realize the hopelessness of their mission. They returned.

At this time it seemed to Captain Sigsbee that a long interval had elapsed since the explosion, but actually it had been a matter of minutes. Sigsbee's vision was only now becoming adapted.

"One of the smokestacks was lying in the water on the starboard side," he said later. "Although it was almost directly under me, I had not at first identified it. I could see white forms on the water and hear faint cries for help."

The captain was relieved to observe the three boats in the water rescuing sailors.

Ambrose Ham had helped lower the gig. He had been on the poop deck the entire time and had seen Sigsbee and the other officers come up from the main deck.

"We had a little trouble," Ham said, "as the ship listed to port. But finally we got the boat in the water." As the boat was being lowered, Ham jumped into it to help get it water-borne.

He heard Lieutenant Blow, who was handling the forward fall, call down to him, "Is everything all right?"

Ham answered affirmatively, not knowing Blow's reason for asking. The lieutenant observed that the gig had been lowered only six feet or so and presumed it was hanging out of the water. Perhaps, thought the lieutenant, the blocks had jammed.

"Why won't the boat go down?" Blow asked. Ham answered that it was already afloat.

Near Ham, while he had helped lower the gig, had

From Harper's Weekly

On November 18, 1890, twenty thousand persons packed the navy yard at Brooklyn to see the hull of the *Maine* launched.

Official U.S. Navy Photograph

Five years after launching, the ship was ready for sea. The sides were painted a glittering white, the superstructure ochre.

RECORD OF THE MISCELLANEOUS EVENTS OF THE DAY.

Meridian to 4 P.M. At 2 P.M. the officers and crew having been assembled on board and mustered aft, the National Ensign was run up to the peak: then saluted & the colors was sounded by the music and the pennant was broken at the main truck. Captain A. S. Crowninshield read his orders from the Navy Department assigning him to the command of the U. S. Steel armored Cruiser Maine 1st Rate. Captain Frederick Rodgers, Captain of the New York Navy Yard turned the vessel over to Captain Crowninshield. The following officers were on board for duty. (See opposite page)

Geo. L. W. Johnson
Lieut. U. S. N.
Navigator & Ordnance Officer

4 P.M. to Midnight. Clear and pleasant, light variable breezes from 2. to 7. Afterwards light breeze from South.

Bowers N. Galt
Lieut. U. S. N.

Examined and found to be correct.

Geo. L. W. Johnson
Lieut. U. S. N. V.   Navigation

The first entry in the log of the *Maine* was made at 4:00 P.M. on September 17, 1895, two hours after the commissioning ceremony.

Harper's Weekly

These two pictures depict the *Maine* in action. Above is a somewhat inaccurate portrayal of North Atlantic Squadron maneuvers. In the foreground is the superstructure of the *Massachusetts*. In the background, from left to right, are the *Maine, New York, Indiana,* and *Iowa*. Below is an artist's conception of the *Maine* during the storm of February 5 and 6, 1897. Five men were swept overboard; the two men shown clinging to the life buoy were rescued.

National Archives

Captain Charles D. Sigsbee, who assumed command of the *Maine* April 10, 1897. On the same day, his commission as captain was signed.

Seaman Mike Flynn, a British navy veteran. He enjoyed his duty on the *Maine* after serving aboard the more strictly disciplined English ships.

Apprentice Ambrose Ham of Schenectady, New York. This picture was taken a few months after the explosion, when he was on the *Marblehead*.

Ambrose Ham (standing, fifth from left) sang in the Bachelor's Glee Club. Second from left, reclining, is the apprentice with whom Ham exchanged duty. The switch was to cost the boy, whose name Ham does not remember, his life.

Sole survivor of the *Maine* baseball team was Landsman John H. Bloomer of East Deering, Maine (back row, far left). Bugler C. H. Newton of Washington, D.C., is second from left in the second row. The goat (foreground) was left in Key West.

The *Maine* was ready for battle when it passed Morro Castle at 9:30 A.M., January 25, 1898. The ship had been ordered to Havana to protect United States citizens there.

Upon mooring at Havana, Captain Sigsbee sent this one-word arrival report to the Bureau of Navigation.

Official U.S. Navy Photograph

This faded photograph was the last one taken of the *Maine* before the disaster. It was snapped at 4:00 P.M. February 15, 1898. At 9:40 o'clock that night the ship blew up.

An artist's conception of the tragedy shows this scene on the ruined *Maine* shortly before Captain Sigsbee ordered, "Get into the boats, gentlemen."

Author's Collection

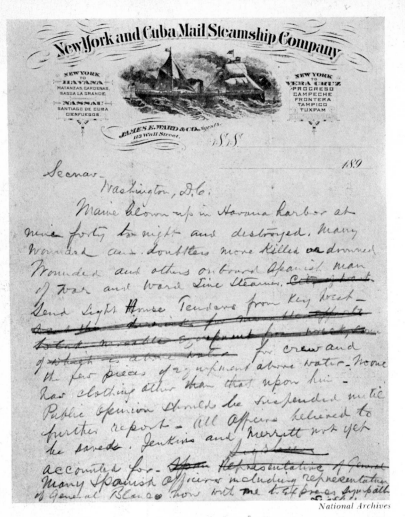

Shortly after the explosion Captain Sigsbee wrote this report to the Secretary of the Navy. He used stationery borrowed from Captain Frank Stevens of the American steamship *City of Washington*. *Harper's Weekly* correspondent George Bronson Rea carried the dispatch ashore to the Havana cable office, where it was sent to Washington.

(*opposite*) After the tragedy a twisted mass of wreckage protruded from the water, marking the spot where the *Maine* had exploded. Seaman Mike Flynn's hammock was in this part of the ship.

Navy divers sent down to investigate the wreck for the court of inquiry recovered the cipher code and the magazine keys. Later they discovered hull plates that were bent inward.

Six and one-half years after the Spanish-American War had ended, the wreck of the *Maine* was still visible in Havana harbor. This picture was taken in 1905.

In 1911 the Army Corps of Engineers began the work of raising the *Maine*. They first planted a cofferdam around the wreck and pumped out the water.

Engineers discovered the sternmost portion of the wreck in surprisingly good condition. The turret shown is the after ten-inch, on the port side.

At this spot members of the second court of inquiry found plates bent inward, suggesting an external explosion. One plate is marked with a white line.

In a solemn funeral procession in March, 1912, Cuban soldiers carried coffins containing the remains of an estimated sixty-four *Maine* crewmen. They had been removed from the exposed wreck fourteen years after the explosion.

When the funeral procession halted at the wharf, former *Maine* Chaplain John P. Chidwick (not shown) spoke briefly. Then the caskets were transferred to the *U.S.S. North Carolina.*

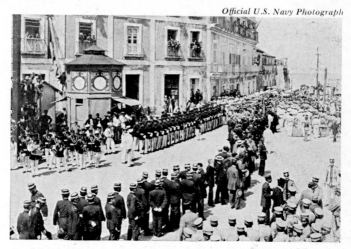

From the *North Carolina* the remains of the *Maine* victims were transferred to the *Birmingham*, a smaller vessel, which transported them to Washington, D.C. This is a photograph of a memorial service on the *Birmingham* fantail.

The last *Maine* crewmen arrived home fourteen years after the explosion. Here are their caskets being taken from the *Birmingham* for burial in Arlington National Cemetery.

While a warship fired a gun every mile of the way, the wreck of the *Maine* was taken to sea for sinking. The vessel showing smoke is the tug *Osceola*, towing the hulk.

The *Maine,* abandoned with sea cocks open, began sinking slowly at first. A newspaper reporter observed, "The vessel appeared to fight against her fate."

The hulk plunged downward about 5:30 P.M. March 16, 1912, with the huge ensign vanishing "under a sea of foam with a flash of red, white, and blue." The final resting place of the *Maine* was in 600 fathoms of water.

Two former crew members who remember the *Maine* are (left) Michael J. Flynn of Philadelphia and (right) Ambrose Ham, now of Binghamton, New York.

The salvaged commission pennant and boat ensign of the *Maine* were returned to the Navy in a ceremony on February 15, 1956. Left to right are Rear Admiral Roscoe H. Hillenkoetter, who accepted the flags for the Navy; Gustave J. Dressler and Alonzo Willis, survivors of the explosion; John Everetts, Sr., donor of the flags; Governor Edmund Muskie of Maine; and Chief Petty Officer Frank R. Himes, official escort for Mr. Everetts.

stood Chaplain Chidwick, horrified by what he saw. His first impression was that "a war was on; that the enemy had engaged us and that the deck would be swept by shells and bullets."

Chidwick also heard the urgent cries for help from men in the water.

"Immediately I gave them absolution. I called upon the men to mention the name of Jesus, and again and again I repeated the absolution." Next morning several persons who had watched the tragedy from ashore were to tell Chidwick that they had heard his words. He commented, "I only hope some of the men heard."

Chidwick's altar boy, Ordinary Seaman Frederick C. Holzer, came to him crying.

"Look at me, Father," he implored. "I'm all burned." But Chidwick had no time to talk. He ordered Holzer (who died ten days later) into a boat.

Then from the barge, which had been lowered, Chidwick heard the voice of Lieutenant Jungen.

"I think we can do better work, Chaplain, by rowing around to pick up some of the men."

Chidwick jumped into the boat, which now was not far below the level of the poop deck. Six others were already in the boat—Jungen, Lieutenant Catlin, Assistant Engineer John R. Morris, and three enlisted men. One of the men was the poop-deck sentry, who after the explosion had calmly remembered orders given him to load his rifle in case of emergency. When he leaped into the boat the weapon was ready to fire.

Following Chidwick, two other officers jumped into the barge—Paymaster Charles M. Ray and Lieutenant Blow. Then Jungen, senior officer in the boat, directed it around the starboard side of the *Maine*. Most of the others, enlisted men and officers alike, manned oars.

They pulled around the wreckage, which reminded Jungen of the dense driftwood he had seen in the Mississippi River during the '97 Mardi Gras visit. They observed that water appeared to be flowing through the *Maine* amidships. Forward of this spot they saw a fiery mass of wreckage and, in the water near the inferno, a man struggling to save himself. Jungen took the boat in long enough to haul him aboard.

Several other boats, including many manned by Spaniards, searched for survivors in the water.

One boat—from the *City of Washington*—attracted the attention of Master-at-Arms Load. He called to it, but Naval Cadet Bronson, in charge of a whaleboat nearby, replied that he would help instead. Bronson's boat had just picked up Thompson, the marine corporal who had been blown through the awning.

"Throw me your painter!" Load yelled from the deck to Bronson. Load caught it and made it fast to a nearby cradle. Then he lowered several injured men into the water so they could swim to the boat.

Private Lutz, whom Load had rescued from the flaming awning, called:

"Give me some help here. There are two men dying."

Load helped Lutz carry the two sailors to the rail. They dropped them into the water; there was no better way. Seaman Andrew V. Erikson, who earlier had written a friend that "there is liable to be trouble at any time," was hauled into the boat immediately. But Seaman Carl A. Smith, a native of Germany, fell short of the grasp of the boat crew. Cadet Bronson jumped into the water, swam to Smith, and tugged him into the boat. Three days later Erikson and Smith died in a Havana hospital.

Load himself then determined to swim for the boat, but while walking to a more favorable spot from which to dive he slipped and fell overboard. A Spanish shore boat picked him up. The same boat later rescued Seaman Rau, who had been in the steam launch when it capsized, and Fireman Second Class Michael Malone. But Malone, badly injured, fell out of the boat and drowned before anyone could reach him.

Captain Sigsbee and several others were still standing on the poop deck when the barge returned to the ship. Jungen invited Sigsbee to step into the barge, but the captain declined. He said he would use his gig.

Ambrose Ham had stationed himself in the bow of the gig while it was rowed in the vicinity of the wreck. He and the others had pulled several men out of the water. But, all the while, Ham was extremely anxious about another magazine explosion. He wished one of the officers would order the boat away from the ship.

Two of the men Ham helped rescue were Coal Passer Melville and Seaman McCann. Earlier, Melville, McCann, and Wilbur had made their way aft from the starboard gangway to a whaleboat, had seen that it was not serviceable, and were returning to the gangway when Wilbur fell—or jumped—overboard and disappeared. (A boat picked him up and took him to a hospital ashore. He later told his two companions that he had fallen overboard, but he told the court of inquiry that he had seen a Spanish boat lying off, had jumped in and swum for it.)

Melville and McCann noticed the gig nearby. The coxswain, they observed, was shouting for them to dive overboard and swim to the boat. They jumped immediately.

Soon after the two were helped aboard, the coxswain heard Private Anthony, Sigsbee's orderly, call for the gig, and he brought it alongside the after part of the poop deck.

Even today Ambrose Ham remembers how reluctant Captain Sigsbee was to step from the ship into the gig.

"I won't leave," Ham remembers the captain as saying, "until I'm sure everybody is off."

But Lieutenant Commander Wainwright whispered to the captain that the inferno forward was endangering the ten-inch magazine.

"Captain," he said, "we'd better leave her."

Sigsbee, after a reflective pause, gave the order to abandon ship.

"Get into the boats, gentlemen," he said.

While some persons in the group around Sigsbee stepped into the boats alongside, a sailor picked up the captain's dog, Peggy, that had somehow found her master in all the excitement. He handed her to a man in the gig crew. Then the sailor himself stepped into the gig.

The after part of the poop deck, highest part of the ship above water, was now level with the gunwale of the gig; but Wainwright and Lieutenant Holman, standing beside Sigsbee, offered the captain a hand.

Sigsbee hesitated, pointing out that he should leave the ship last. The two other officers stepped into the gig, and Sigsbee followed. The captain informed the crews of several other boats clustered around the stern that they should leave the vicinity. Then the gig crew pulled for the *City of Washington*.

The *Maine*, abandoned at last, burned furiously and settled deeper into the mud, while explosions of ammunition continued to rock her from time to time.

While Sigsbee was being rowed to the *City of Washington*, *Harper's Weekly* correspondent George Bronson Rea and Sylvester Scovel, a reporter for the *New York World*, followed him in another boat.

Rea had been at a Havana café with Mr. and Mrs. Scovel

when they were startled by the sound of "a terrible explosion" that shattered several windows in the city. As the three excited persons rose from their chairs Rea observed an "intense light" in the sky toward the harbor. He had waited while Scovel saw his wife safely off to the apartment; then the two men jumped into a coach and ordered its reluctant driver to proceed in the direction of the docks.

Havana streets, Rea discovered, were surprisingly free of people. He reasoned that the citizens must have feared that the explosion was the forerunner of another riot and fled indoors.

"But as we approached the docks the excitement increased, and when we reached the customhouse gate we found a crowd trying to force its way through, despite the resistance of the guards."

The two men jumped out of their coach. Rea tossed the driver a coin, and they elbowed through the crowd. From the talk, they realized that the explosion had occurred on board the *Maine*.

At the gate they convinced a guard that they were officers from the United States warship. (Such statements by these two and other reporters later led to rumors that most of the *Maine* officers were ashore that night.) The gate was opened for them and hurriedly slammed shut against the pressing crowd. They raced through the baggage-inspection room and out onto the open wharf. Then they saw the *Maine* burning furiously.

The police chief of Havana, Colonel Paglieri, offered the two Americans a ride in his boat, which was ready to shove off, and they unceremoniously jumped into it.

"Our boatmen were paralyzed with fear and wished to turn back," Rea said. "The colonel beat one of them with his cane. I whacked the other with a rope's end." These

THE FATE OF THE "MAINE"

persuasive measures proved effective enough to get them
to the immediate vicinity of the *Maine*, and Rea was
aghast at what he saw.

"Great masses of twisted and bent iron plates and
beams were thrown up in confusion amidships. The bow
had disappeared. The foremast and smokestacks had fallen,
and to add to the horror, the mass of wreckage amidships was on fire. At frequent intervals a loud report,
followed by the whistling sound of a fragment flying
through the air, marked the explosion of a six-inch shell."

Another American had seen the excitement ashore.
Charles H. Pearson, a member of the Produce Exchange
of New York City, had been standing in front of the
Hotel Inglaterra downtown, watching the passing crowd,
when he heard the explosion.

The people, he observed, became excited, almost panicky. Some believed that another riot had broken out.
Others, Pearson said, believed the fast-spreading rumors
that the *Maine* was bombarding Havana.

"As soon as the truth became known," Pearson said,
"there was a strong feeling of horror and sadness."

7

A Time for Sympathy

The President directs all colors to be half-masted until further orders account of disaster to the *Maine*.

—Secretary Long,
to all ships and stations

Ambrose Ham cast side glances at his captain as Ham helped row the gig to the *City of Washington*. He observed that Sigsbee was "cool, but changed. He looked ten years older."

Sigsbee, however, still had his wits about him. He called again to other boats to leave the vicinity of the wreck before another explosion occurred. Seeing Scovel, an acquaintance, in the boat with Rea and the Havana police chief, Sigsbee asked that Scovel translate this advice for the Spanish boats.

After the gig had arrived alongside the American

steamer, Ham followed Sigsbee and the other officers up the gangway. Rain began to fall, and they hurried inside. Ham walked to a makeshift hospital in the saloon for treatment of injuries, and he was appalled at what he saw.

"Nearly twenty of our men were getting their injuries attended to," he said. "Some had no clothes on and were burned all over."

They lay on mattresses, hurriedly carried to the saloon by officers and crewmen of the *City of Washington* after the explosion. Captain Sigsbee walked among the injured men for several minutes; then he stepped out on deck and stood at the rail. The rain had stopped, and he watched explosions of ammunition aboard his ship. Sigsbee saw that the *Maine* rested on the bottom of the harbor now but that it was still burning.

He retired then to the captain's cabin, made available to him by Captain Frank Stevens. He sat at Stevens' desk and composed a telegram to the Navy Department.

"Secnav—Washington, D.C.," he scribbled with a pencil. "*Maine* blown up in Havana harbor at nine forty tonight and destroyed. Many wounded and doubtless more killed or drowned. Wounded and others on board Spanish man of war and Ward Line steamer. Send light house tenders from Key West . . ."

He wrote a few words after that, thought better, lined through them, and continued, ". . . for crew and the few pieces of equipment above water. No one has clothing other than that upon him. Public opinion should be suspended until further report. All officers believed to be saved. Jenkins and Merritt not yet accounted for."

Sigsbee had signed the telegram when a messenger knocked and informed him that several Spanish officials were on board to express their sympathy.

Sigsbee put the pencil on the desk and went on deck to receive them: Cuban Secretary General Congosto, chief of staff to Governor General Blanco; the Havana police chief, with whom Rea and Scovel had visited the vicinity of the wreck; and others. Rea and Scovel also were present.

Sigsbee heard the Spaniards voice their regret. Thanking them, he excused himself for a few minutes to complete the telegram.

He lined out his name at the bottom of the message and added the words, "Many Spanish officers including representative of General Blanco now with me to express sympathy." Then he signed his name again.

He called Secretary General Congosto into the cabin and read the wire to him. Congosto, a former Spanish consul in the United States, remarked that the wording was "very kind." Congosto promised that the closed cable office would be reopened for sending the message, and Sigsbee gave it to correspondent Rea with the request that Rea take it to the cable office.

Sigsbee also scribbled a shorter dispatch.

"Forsyth—Key West. Tell admiral *Maine* blown up and destroyed. Send light house tenders. Many killed and wounded. Don't send war vessels if others available. Sigsbee."

Rea, of course, was happy to perform the service of seeing that the dispatches were sent. He placed them with a stack of cable messages from about forty other officers and men by that time on the *City of Washington*, and he departed with Scovel and the party of Spaniards.

Later Rea was to send the original of the longer wire to a newspaper, which reproduced the document and returned it to Rea. Then he returned it to Sigsbee, who kept it for several years before giving it to the National

Archives, where it remains today, forgotten in a filing envelope with fifty or sixty other old naval dispatches. Clipped to it is a request, in Sigsbee's handwriting, to use the dispatch in full if it is used at all.

After the Spaniards had departed, Sigsbee granted Chaplain Chidwick permission to go ashore to see about the injured men there. Then Sigsbee watched the periodic explosions of ammunition on board the *Maine* until 1:30 A.M., when he retired.

"It was indeed a sorry night," he said. "There was a stench in the air from the foul water of the harbor. I knew that weeks of difficulty would begin early the next morning. Nevertheless, I slept and got some of the rest so much needed for preparation."

While Sigsbee slept, Chidwick visited Havana hospitals, took names of victims, and returned in the early-morning hours. Lieutenant Commander Wainwright, meanwhile, had conducted a muster of survivors on the *City of Washington* and the *Alfonso XII*. The result of this was the discovery that of twenty-two officers (four others were ashore that night) and 328 men, 252 were dead or missing. Eight survivors were to die in Havana hospitals during the next few days.

After Wainwright had completed the muster, he and Lieutenant Holman embarked in the gig for a closer look at the wreck. A Spanish boat patrolling the vicinity waved them off. No one could board the *Maine*, the Spaniards said, without permission from Admiral Manterola. Informed of the Spanish action, Sigsbee went over the admiral's head with a protest—to Captain General Blanco, who immediately granted *Maine* personnel permission to board the wreck. They were greeted by Tom, the crew's pet cat, which had somehow survived the explosion.

In Schenectady, New York, funeral arrangements for Apprentice Ambrose Ham were made by his father. Young Ham had been reported missing.

And in Philadelphia, Seaman Mike Flynn's aunt, Mrs. Maggie Flanagan, had been informed that Flynn was dead. She was not to know otherwise until her nephew shocked her by coming home on leave several weeks later.

A friend of the Ham family suggested that an inquiry be made to be certain that Ambrose was dead. Back came a wire. The report was incorrect, it said. Apprentice Ham was in a hospital at Key West, minus a tooth and with a deep gash an inch above his left eye.

Ham had been sent to Key West on Wednesday, the day after the explosion. Early that morning he had stood leaning on the rail of the *City of Washington*, wistfully gazing at the ruined *Maine*. The poop deck, above water the night before when Captain Sigsbee had stepped from it into his gig, now was submerged, Ham observed.

With the *City of Washington* scheduled to depart later that same Wednesday for Vera Cruz, many of the injured sailors, including Ambrose Ham, were transferred to the *Olivette* and transported that afternoon to Key West. Other crew members were in such critical condition, however, that they were sent to Havana hospitals.

As the *Olivette* steamed past Morro Castle at 2:30 P.M., Ham thought "how different things were. We had entered in as fine a ship as ever sailed; but now we were leaving, burned and injured, and in a ship that could not fight—that probably would have been sunk by a single shot."

Shortly before midnight that February 16 the *Olivette* reached Key West. The injured sailors were greeted by a large crowd of citizens who had heard that the *Maine* survivors were due to arrive.

The Secretary of the Navy, meanwhile, had ordered the men kept there indefinitely for observation of yellow fever.

"Some were taken to the Marine Hospital," Ham wrote, "but I went to the Army Hospital. We had nice beds to sleep in and good food. The stewards and nurses did all in their power to help. Almost every day we received fruit and cake from some kind-hearted lady."

Although Ham's troubles were now vanishing, Captain Sigsbee's were just beginning.

Sigsbee had remained in Havana as United States representative in connection with the tragedy. He had sent on the *Olivette*, with Ham, every officer and man able to travel, with the exception of nine: Lieutenant Commander Wainwright, Paymaster Ray, Surgeon Lucien G. Heneberger, Chaplain Chidwick, Lieutenant Holman, Naval Cadets Holden and Cluverius, Private Anthony (the orderly), and Gunner's Mate Second Class Charles H. Bullock of Newburgh, New York. This staff was to assist him in Havana.

Two of Captain Sigsbee's first concerns were for the cipher code and the keys to the magazines, where the ammunition was stowed. Both had gone down with the ship.

Recovery of the cipher code was urgent; possession of this device would enable others to decode encrypted U. S. Navy dispatches. Finding the keys, which had hung at the foot of the captain's bunk, could help prove that the magazines had indeed been secure on the night of the tragedy.

In a coded telegram sent twelve hours after the explosion (but not made public until much later) Sigsbee requested the services of divers to recover the two items as soon as possible. He added a statement about the cause of the explosion.

"Cipher code sunk with *Maine* but [can be] easily recovered by divers. For that reason American wreckers desirable. *Maine* was probably destroyed by a mine. It may have been done by accident. I surmise that her berth was planted previous to her arrival; perhaps long ago. I can only surmise this."

In his first dispatch Sigsbee had urged that public opinion be suspended, but this was not possible. To most Americans there was no doubt about the conclusion to be drawn from the fact that the *Maine* had been destroyed at night in a Spanish port. As retired Rear Admiral George E. Belknap said, it was significant that the ship should have blown up "in that particular harbor at this particular time."

The commandant of the Portsmouth Navy Yard, George C. R. Memmey, was moved to wire the chief of the Bureau of Navigation, "If inspection shows external explosion, suggest seizing Spanish torpedo boats now in the Atlantic."

From London came the opinion of Hiram Stevens Maxim, manufacturer of guns bearing his name, that a torpedo exploding under the *Maine,* in close contact with the ship, could ignite the inflammables inside.

John H. Burnell of Opelika, Alabama, was—like millions of Americans—more adamant. Among the letters flooding the office of Secretary Long was one from him.

"I see it stated that a Spanish pilot placed the battleship *Maine* in her position," he wrote. "More than probable over a mine previously prepared."

But in Madrid, General Weyler snorted a belief that the explosion of the ship was due "to the indolence of her crew."

Another Spaniard denied that his countrymen were

responsible. Señor Dupuy de Lôme, Madrid's envoy to
the United States, had first learned of the disaster from
New York reporters shortly after the news arrived there.
At first he refused to believe the information, but when
he had been convinced of its truth he declared that no
Spaniard would be guilty of such an act.

Ironically, De Lôme was on his way home for good.
Earlier in February he had made many Americans fighting mad with disparaging references to President Mc-
Kinley. The remarks had been made in a private letter
to a friend in Cuba which somehow had found its way into
Hearst's *New York Journal*. Probably the letter had been
taken from the friend's apartment by someone sympathetic to the insurgents and brought to the United
States for propaganda purposes.

De Lôme was aghast when the letter was published.
At first he denied having written it, but it became evident
beyond a doubt that he was the author. Still, his statements
concerning McKinley could not match some of Theodore
Roosevelt's, who commented on one occasion (when Mc-
Kinley seemed too peaceful for Teddy) that the President
had no more backbone than a chocolate éclair. But De
Lôme represented a foreign government—Spain at that
—and American resentment had forced him to telegraph
his resignation to Madrid on February 9.

Other Spaniards besides De Lôme expressed their profound grief over the disaster. Two days after the tragedy
Havana authorities assumed charge of burying the first
nineteen victims whose bodies had been recovered.

"The utmost sympathy and respect were shown," reported Captain Sigsbee.

Some Americans voiced a neutral opinion as to the
cause of the explosion, but they were a minority. When a

reporter asked Secretary Long if he had any reason to suspect that the disaster was the work of an enemy, he replied, "I do not. In that I am influenced by the fact that Captain Sigsbee has not reported to the Navy Department on the cause. So long as he does not express himself, I certainly cannot."

The Army and Navy Journal commented on February 19 that "the combination of steam, electricity, high explosives, and coal that may become self-igniting is not a happy one, and the most exact precautions against accidents may fail at times, as they have in the case of other vessels."

One of the vessels to which the *Journal* referred was the *Cincinnati*. That ship had had its coal fired by spontaneous combustion in 1896 while at Key West. The steel bulkhead separating the bunker from a magazine became hot enough to char shells before someone noticed the danger. The magazines were flooded immediately.

Several years before that, a British warship, the *Dotterel*, had been destroyed by a mysterious explosion in the Strait of Magellan. The origin was traced to a paint room, where inflammable gas apparently had been generated.

With these and other possibilities in mind, *Harper's Weekly* urged that Americans refrain from hostile speech. The editor voiced a hope that the loss of the *Maine* could be proved to have been an accident. Most Americans, however, were ready to fight.

While the discussion of the probable cause of the explosion went on, the Spanish cruiser *Vizcaya* steamed toward New York, her crew ignorant of the tragic event in Havana Harbor. This was, of course, before the days of wireless radio.

The *Vizcaya* had been ordered from Cartagena by an

irked Spanish foreign office to return the "friendly visit" of the *Maine*. She arrived at New York on February 18 and anchored for the night outside the bar.

That same day a man in Lead, South Dakota, telegraphed Secretary Long another typical sentiment.

"Suggest holding Spanish battleship *Vizcaya* for the present in outer New York harbor within range dynamite gun. L. C. Twombly."

Lieutenant Aaron Ward, an aide to Rear Admiral Bunce, who was then commandant of the New York Navy Yard, boarded the *Vizcaya* to offer the usual civilities. He told Captain Antonio Eulate about the fate of the *Maine*.

The Spanish captain was shocked. Immediately he ordered the colors half-masted, and he told Ward they would remain that way during his stay.

Eulate also expressed "extreme regret" at the news. Later, when he visited Admiral Bunce, he said he would not take part in any festivities planned in his honor.

To prevent a similar happening to the *Vizcaya*, the New York Police Department supervised a twenty-four-hour watch on the ship.

Thirteen hundred miles south, Havana was becoming somewhat quieter. United States divers already were at work on the *Maine*.

Their first assignment was to recover the cipher code and the keys to the magazines. This proved to be a difficult task.

The muddy bottom of the harbor was so dark that the divers were forced to grope their way around. They were unable to see anything near the bottom. Making their work even more difficult was their gear: an air hose and a lifeline, lead-soled shoes weighing twenty pounds each, and a lead belt of eighty pounds. Despite the handicaps, however, the cipher code was recovered.

Then Martin Reden, a seaman by rate, dived for the magazine keys. By feeling around he found his way to the captain's cabin and to the bunk. Instructed to search for the keys at the foot of it, he explored the vicinity but found nothing. After his unsuccessful dive he surfaced and reported that the key bag was not there.

"This gave me more of a shock than the explosion itself," Sigsbee said. "A missing key might have meant that a magazine had been entered against my knowledge or that some [Spanish] diver had been down at night and secured the key."

Gunner's Mate Second Class W. H. F. Schluter, from the *New York*, went down to take another look. He reached the captain's bunk and felt at the foot.

No keys. Reden had been right.

Then Schluter felt inside the bunk itself and discovered that there was no mattress. He realized that it must have floated off when the ship sank.

Schluter raised his arms, and above him he felt the mattress. It was pressed against the overhead, directly over the bunk.

He felt around the mattress then and touched an object. Carefully retrieving it, he discovered that it was the missing key bag. The mattress had snagged it during the rise to the overhead when the ship sank.

Schluter gripped the bag firmly and signaled that he was returning to the surface. Lieutenant Holman, ordnance officer and navigator of the *Maine*, looked through the bag and found the key to every magazine and shell room.

"My relief," Sigsbee said, "was very great."

8

The Inquiry

There is no evidence that the disaster was the work of
an enemy . . . but [there is] a harsh note of suspicion
of murderous treachery.

—*Harper's Weekly*

Members of the United States court of inquiry arrived at
Havana on the U.S.S. *Mangrove* on February 21—six
days after the disaster. Whether or not there would be
war seemed to hinge on what this court decided about the
cause of the explosion.

The senior member, Captain (soon to be Admiral)
William T. Sampson, was accompanied by Captain Chadwick of the flagship *New York* and Lieutenant Commander William P. Potter, Chadwick's executive officer.
Lieutenant Commander Adolph Marix, former executive
officer of the *Maine*, served as judge advocate.

The court was to meet in strict secrecy. Newsmen were not to be allowed on board the *Mangrove*.

Meanwhile, a Spanish court—Captain Don Pedro del Peral y Caballero, judge, and Lieutenant Don Javier de Salas y Gonzales, secretary—had begun questioning witnesses immediately after the explosion.

The first witness called by the United States court, Captain Sigsbee, lost no time volunteering information on a subject being discussed around the world: had the berth been mined before the arrival of the *Maine?*

Sigsbee testified that Captain Stevens of the *City of Washington* told him the buoy to which the *Maine* had been moored was the least used of any in the harbor.

"I have been informed that he had never known a man-of-war to be anchored at that buoy," Sigsbee testified, "and that he had rarely known merchant vessels to be anchored there."

Strangely enough, no member of the court was to query Stevens about this when he appeared later as a witness, and no other effort was made to verify the information. The fact was that the buoy had not been used often by warships, but merchant vessels had moored to it rather frequently.

With Sigsbee's initial testimony taken, the court went to work to discover any evidence of negligence on the part of *Maine* personnel.

The logical reason for the tragedy, presuming an internal explosion, was spontaneous combustion—of coal, paint, or other inflammables. This could have brought about an explosion of the magazines.

Perhaps coal in a bunker near one of the magazines had begun to smolder. The heat might have exploded the powder. One of the first questions Sigsbee was asked concerned this possibility.

"Did you ever receive any report from the chief engineer of your ship that any coal had been too long in any bunker?"

"Never that I can recollect," Sigsbee answered.

"Did the fire alarms in the bunkers work?"

"They were sensitive. They worked occasionally when there was no undue heat in the bunkers, on which occasions we invariably examined the bunkers and got a report."

Daily logs of the *Maine* kept in the National Archives indeed state that on at least two occasions—June 14, 1896, and July 11, 1897—this had happened, and it probably occurred more often than twice.

The coal bunkers were, however, still under suspicion, especially the forward bunkers nearest the magazines. The fire alarm system might have failed to work.

Chief Engineer Howell was called to provide detailed information on the bunkers. He enumerated those in the forward section.

"On the starboard side, adjacent to the ten-inch magazine, are coal bunkers A15, B3, and B5. On the port side, adjacent to the six-inch reserve magazine, are coal bunkers A16, B4, and B6." To naval personnel odd numbers mean starboard, even numbers port.

Howell then explained that A15 was a difficult bunker to fill or to empty, because "you have to go through B3 and B5. To take coal out of A15 you first have to empty B3 and B5, and to put coal in A15 you have to partially fill B5, and then fill from B5 into A15."

A similar arrangement existed on the port side, where A16 was the difficult bunker to reach.

Here, then, was a possibility: could not the coal in A15 or A16 have become ignited, perhaps have smoldered for days, and heated the magazines enough to explode their contents? Since these bunkers were difficult to reach, this might have occurred without anyone's noticing the danger.

"Have you had any signs of spontaneous combustion in the coal bunkers?" Howell was asked.

"No, sir; none whatever."

"When did you make your last examination of these bunkers?"

"Bunkers B3, B5, B4, and B6 were empty, and they had been empty about two weeks. In that time we had scaled and painted all those bunkers. Also, we had scaled and painted the chute that led down to them." The chief engineer added that the chutes had been left open and that these bunkers were ventilated by air pipes.

A15, Howell continued, was being used at the time of the explosion. At 4:00 P.M. on February 15 his engineer force had begun taking coal from A15 to keep the ship on an even trim.

The starboard bunkers, then, were cleared of suspicion. The questioning shifted to those on the port side.

"At the time of the explosion what was the condition of bunker A16?" This was the one adjacent to the six-inch reserve magazine.

"It was full of coal."

But then Captain Sigsbee, who sat in on most sessions, questioned his chief engineer to bring out a fact: the outer bulkhead of bunker A16 was exposed at the forward entrance of the port-wing passage, and the hands of the crew probably touched the bunker many times every day. If any man had noticed heat, Sigsbee reasoned, he would have reported it.

"There was a turn to the left in that passageway," Sigsbee explained afterward. "On three sides of this turn the plating of the bunker was exposed. The passage was narrow. The tendency, therefore, of a person turning to the left would have been to place his left hand on the plating."

Later that same day Sigsbee himself returned as a witness to say that he had walked through that very passage "either the day before or two days before—I think the day before the explosion." He had put his hand on the plating and did not remember that it was unusually warm.

When the engineer watch officer, John R. Morris, was called as a witness most of the remaining suspicion of the bunkers vanished.

Morris told the court that he had inspected the bunkers, including A16, about eleven hours before the explosion. He found them in good condition.

Still later, Schluter, the diver who had retrieved the magazine keys, testified that during one descent he had landed in a pile of coal. He inspected it as carefully as possible, he said, and found nothing wrong with it. At that time he was in the forward part of the submerged ship, where the explosion had occurred.

Even the pile from which the *Maine* had last taken coal (at Key West) was examined piece by piece, although an engineer officer had inspected it at the time of coaling.

Machinist Charles Goodwin of the naval station at Key West had charge of this work. He supervised a gang of shovelers who sifted the thousand-ton pile literally lump by lump. Two other inspectors assisted Goodwin, but they discovered nothing unusual.

If the bunkers were free of suspicion, the electric plant and the boilers were not. Either could have caused the explosion.

Perhaps, suggested some observers, the electric plant

had grounded. But questioning in the court of inquiry brought out the improbability of this. Every witness who offered testimony on the subject said that there had been no disturbance in the lights until they were suddenly extinguished when the explosion wrecked the ship.

The boilers, too, were blameless. The court discovered that only the two aftermost boilers—nowhere near the vicinity of the explosion—had been in use on the night of February 15 and that they were carrying not more than 100 pounds of steam, compared to 120 pounds at sea. Safety valves on both were designed to blow at 130.

Passed Assistant Engineer Frederic C. Bowers had made a routine inspection of the boilers one hour and fifty-five minutes before the ship blew up.

"I looked at the fires and noted the water in the glass," he said. "There was three quarters of a column of water. The boilers were in every way in a normal condition."

Inflammables, also, were cleared of suspicion. Inquiry brought out the information that the painter had been allowed to stow his combustibles only in chests aft. The court even questioned Surgeon Lucien Heneberger about the storage of medical whiskies and brandies, and discovered that they, too, had always been kept aft.

Although the court uncovered nothing to indicate that an internal force had set off a magazine explosion, it did prove conclusively that there had been two blasts.

Captain Sigsbee, however, could recall only one.

"So far as my experience is concerned there was simply one impression of an overwhelming explosion," he said.

Lieutenant Commander Wainwright agreed. He testified that it seemed to him there had been only one "very heavy shock."

Marine Private Anthony, the captain's orderly, also heard only one explosion.

"I first noticed a trembling and buckling of the decks, and then this prolonged roar—not a short report, but a prolonged roar. The awnings were spread, and where the wing awning and the quarter-deck awning join there was a space of at least eighteen inches. I looked out and saw an immense sheet of flame. Then I started in to warn the captain."

But most of the survivors testified that there had been two distinct explosions.

Naval Cadet Cluverius felt "a slight shock as if a six-pounder had been fired somewhere about the deck." After that he heard and felt a mammoth explosion.

Another naval cadet, Jonas H. Holden, also recalled hearing two detonations. "First there was an explosion of considerable force, and about three or four seconds later there was a far greater explosion."

Chief Engineer Howell, while sitting in the wardroom with Lieutenants Holman, Jungen, and Jenkins, had been startled by "an unusual shock, a continued series of convulsions, and a noise as if the ship was being torn to pieces —then a tremendous crash."

Lieutenant Hood, who had been chatting with officer of the deck Blandin, was certain that there had been two explosions.

"I felt more than I heard the first one," he said. "It sounded and felt like an underwater explosion. The instant I turned my head to look forward there was a second explosion."

Hood said he then saw the forward deck blow up. It seemed to be hurtling in his direction, a fiery mass of metal. He sprang behind the after edge of the superstructure.

Lieutenant Blow agreed that there had been two shocks. At the first one he had rushed out of his room to learn the cause.

"Before I could get more than six feet from my room," he recalled, "a second and much more violent explosion followed." Blow's first thought had been that the *Maine* was being fired on, and he was surprised that it was by such a heavy gun.

Seaman Louis Morinière, a native Frenchman, told the court he had been standing on the main deck when he heard a report. The second explosion knocked him fifteen feet aft, and he landed on all fours.

Lieutenant Holman testified that he was certain there had been two explosions. The first noise, he said, was "a low and heavy rumbling." This was followed almost immediately by the second explosion.

Holman volunteered more information.

"It was precisely similar to many other submarine explosions I have heard, except that it was on a much larger scale. A submarine explosion always gives two shocks— one transmitted through the water, the other—the atmospheric shock—immediately following."

This testimony carried much weight with members of the court, because Holman was a specialist in explosives. He had been assigned to that work for several years at the navy's Newport, Rhode Island, station.

Although Holman and others voiced confidence that there had been two explosions, the court members realized that most persons on the ship when it blew up must have been so dazed and shocked they could not really recall the event with complete accuracy. For verification, the investigators summoned several witnesses who had not been aboard the *Maine*.

Two of them were Sigmond Rothschild and Louis

Wertheimer, who related how they had been on the stern of the *City of Washington* when they heard the first noise and saw the *Maine* rise several feet out of the water. Immediately, they said, came the destructive explosion.

Another witness, Captain Frederick G. Teasdale, master of the English bark *Deva*, corroborated the testimony of the two men. The *Deva* at the time had been tied up at a Regla wharf, about half a mile from the *Maine*.

Teasdale told the court he had been sitting in his cabin writing when he heard what seemed to be a shot. He rushed on deck and was there when the second explosion occurred. It shook him and knocked studs out of the sides of the cabin-door transom.

Then Captain Stevens of the *City of Washington* appeared before the court to say that he had heard first a muffled blast, seeming to come from under water. This was followed instantly, he said, by a second explosion.

It was clear, then, that there had been two explosions. But what had caused the first one? Evidently not the electric plant nor the boilers. And after a thorough investigation the coal bunkers and stowed inflammables had been virtually cleared of blame.

The next logical step was a closer study of the forward magazines. Practically everybody in Havana agreed that the second blast, the one that actually destroyed the ship, must have been a magazine explosion.

But the court uncovered not one case of negligence in handling ammunition. Captain Sigsbee had, in fact, been more careful than his predecessor in following safety regulations.

Until Sigsbee assumed command, the gunner's mates had not bothered to wear special slippers (to avoid sparks) when entering the magazines. Sigsbee was aghast when he learned of this laxity. He ordered Lieutenant Holman, as ordnance officer, to have the men wear the footgear required by regulations.

Holman testified that magazine temperatures had been taken daily by Chief Gunner's Mate Arthur Brofeldt, "a thoroughly reliable man." Invariably, the highest reading was from the ten-inch magazine aft, Holman said; occasionally it registered as much as 110 degrees in hot weather. But this magazine had not exploded.

Navy divers now provided some thought-provoking information. During their descents they had discovered that the entire contents of the forward magazines had not blown up. If the explosion had originated from within, would not every shell have been detonated? The alternative was clear: if a mine outside the ship had exploded first, perhaps bursting plates and throwing water into the magazines, it could have prevented some of the ammunition from exploding.

Diver Thomas Smith, from the battleship *Iowa*, found a ten-inch tank still containing powder and brought it to the surface. Similar discoveries were made by other divers.

On one descent, diver Andrew Olsen was able to discern mud of a different color from that he had previously observed. He brought up a sample and dried it. Two members of the court of inquiry experimented. Ignited by a match, the sample burned readily. The smoke had a strong odor of gunpowder.

The investigators, who had first made an honest effort to uncover any possibility of an accidental explosion, now began to think in terms of an external cause. Further discoveries reported by divers encouraged this. At this stage the news leaked to the press.

One correspondent in Havana was Walter Scott Meriwether of the *New York Herald*. Meriwether had served in the United States Navy from 1882 to 1892, and he had made many friends. In 1892 he had left the service to become navy editor of the *New York Times*. Three years later he had moved to the *Herald*, and in January of 1898 he had been assigned to report the operations of the North Atlantic Squadron at Key West.

Meriwether had been in the Florida city when he received this telegram from James Gordon Bennett: "Go Havana. Relieve Caldwell. Tell him come home. Bennett."

John R. Caldwell, the *Herald* man referred to in Bennett's telegram, was out of favor with the Spaniards. He had been extremely critical of General Weyler in his dispatches, and he had been friendly with Fred Funston, an American fighter with the Cuban rebels.

Meriwether went to Havana, and while speculation was rampant about whether the court of inquiry would decide that the explosion was interior or exterior he received a solid tip.

About ten o'clock on an early-March night, Meriwether heard a knock on the door of his hotel room. He opened the door and recognized Gunner Charles Morgan, a former shipmate he had not seen in years.

Morgan, off the *New York*, voiced greetings and quickly entered the room. Meriwether closed the door.

"I'm in charge of the divers," Morgan said, "and we've found the keel of the *Maine* within eighteen inches of the surface. Mr. Powelson [Ensign W. V. N. Powelson] was with me, and he identified the keel plates."

Meriwether realized that this was the biggest news since the explosion. He surmised, as would most other persons, that only a mine under the ship could bend the keel so out of shape that it would rest near the top of the water. But how could he get this news past the Spanish censor tonight?

Meriwether had been ordered by Bennett to ascertain as soon as possible whether the explosion was internal or external. Considering these instructions, the information demanded immediate transmittal.

Spanish censorship in Havana, strict before the explosion, had become even tighter in the weeks following. Every newspaper in Cuba had to be approved before publication, and every dispatch was required to be submitted to a censor. In the case of American correspondents like Meriwether, one copy had to be in English and one translated into Spanish.

The telegraph office sent only dispatches bearing the censor's stamp. But there was one other way for the American newsmen to get stories out of the country. They could leave their dispatches aboard the *Olivette* or other ships bound for Key West. From there the stories could be telegraphed without restriction anywhere in the United States.

Meriwether was more fortunate than most other correspondents. Available for his use was a dispatch boat, although using it now would delay for too long his story.

After Gunner Morgan had departed, Meriwether thumbed through a code book used by *Herald* correspondents in Havana. He found no cipher that would convey the information, so he composed this brief telegram:

"In important story which will be filed from dispatch boat to Key West tomorrow please note that *Maine* story is mine."

When he presented the message to the censor the Spaniard inquired if it was necessary to claim credit for a story not even filed.

Meriwether's affirmative reply was answered with a gruff "You can't—and tell that to your marines." ("His voice wasn't nice," Meriwether recalled half a century later.)

But this particular censor was due to go off duty in a matter of minutes, and as Meriwether left the office he was already thinking of other possibilities. He walked slowly down the darkened Prado to his hotel, there picked up an issue of the old *Life* magazine, and immediately had a code.

When the next censor had come on duty Meriwether again appeared at the office, with this dispatch to the *Herald*:

"Navy contingent left in Havana interestingly reading Kipling's poem current *Life*, especially last verse."

("This was utterly crude," Meriwether said later, "but I thought I might as well try it.")

The censor asked to see the poem. Meriwether handed it to him. It was "The Destroyers," Rudyard Kipling's latest work. The last part of it read:

> *The strength of twice three thousand horse*
> *That serve the one command;*
> *The hand that heaves the headlong force,*
> *The hate that backs the hand:*
> *The doom-bolt in the darkness freed,*
> *The mine that splits the main;*
> *The white-hot wake, the 'wildering speed—*
> *The Choosers of the Slain!*

The censor approved Meriwether's nonsensical dispatch with a frown. Then the *Herald* man went to his room, wrote a detailed story based on Morgan's information, and left it aboard the dispatch vessel for delivery to

Key West the next day. There it was telegraphed to the newspaper.

Sylvester Scovel of the *New York World* also had got wind of the story, but he had no access to a dispatch boat and he was unsuccessful in getting a hint of the story to his paper.

Scovel tried. He filed a lengthy feature on Havana and the harbor, describing the city in generous adjectives, knowing that the Spanish censor would feel flattered. Scovel wrote about the beautiful streets, the colorful stores, and, finally, of the "buzzards roosting on the keel of the *Maine*."

When the cable editor at the *World* read Scovel's story he thought the man had lost his sense of news value. The editor did not reflect on the importance of birds roosting on the keel, and he put the story aside for possible, but not probable, future use. When the *Herald* came out with Meriwether's story the embarrassed cable editor realized his error.

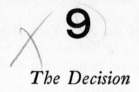

9

The Decision

Of the mysterious cause of the loss of the *Maine* we
are as ignorant as ever. We may never know it; but we
may rest assured that the report of the Sampson Board
of Inquiry will be conclusive. When that is made and
published we shall doubtless know all that ever will be
discovered of the cause of the disaster.

—*Harper's Weekly*

Newspapers of the United States had given their readers
a hint of what to expect from the court of inquiry. But, as
yet, absolutely nothing official had been announced, and
the court continued questioning witnesses.

On March 1 the investigators moved to Key West to in-
terrogate several crew members. Among them was Ambrose Ham, and Ham was somewhat nervous facing all
that gold braid.

Captain Sampson administered the oath to him; then
Judge Advocate Marix began the questioning with the
usual request for full name, rate, and to what ship at-
tached.

Ham answered these questions promptly, managing to conceal most of his excitement.

"Were you on board the *Maine* at the time of her destruction?" Marix asked.

"Yes, sir."

"Tell us exactly where you were at the first intimation of any trouble."

"I was on the starboard side of the poop, near the forward six-pounder."

"Near the forward break of the poop?"

"Yes, sir."

"What were you doing there?"

"I was standing there. I had just been talking to Waters. I don't know his first name. He was a lamplighter."

"What were you doing there? Were you on duty?"

"Yes, sir. I was on duty." Ham, getting a bit flustered now, thought to himself how glad he would be when this questioning ended.

"What duty?"

"Signal duty."

"Tell the court exactly what you felt, heard, and saw of the destruction of the *Maine*."

Ham paused, fidgeted, and began:

"I was standing facing forward, and I was about to turn around when I saw a flash of light—a flame, which seemed to envelop the whole ship—followed by a report." He paused. "I was struck in the face by a flying piece of iron. A perfect hail of flying iron fell all about me. Then the second report.

"I saw the things flying from forward. I didn't know exactly where the second explosion was. After that the officers came up on the poop, and I assisted in lowering the gig."

Ham was trying to be accurate, but he thought to himself after the words had been spoken that he was not at all sure that he had been hit by a "piece of iron." Probably, he decided, by a piece of wood. Still, Ham did not feel like correcting the statement. He heard Marix resume the questioning.

"You speak of two explosions?"

"Yes, sir. It sounded like a roar, the second one."

"What did the first one sound like?"

"It was a sharp report."

"How far were they apart?"

Ham twisted in the chair. He realized that thinking was getting to be almost painful.

"There was only an interval of a couple of seconds."

"Did you feel the ship shake at either explosion?"

"The ship seemed to lift right out of the water."

"At which explosion?"

"At the second explosion."

"Did you feel any trembling or shaking of the ship at the first explosion?"

"No, sir."

"When did you see the flame you speak of?"

"The first thing."

"Before you heard either explosion?"

"Yes, sir."

"One was like a shot and the other like a roar?"

"Yes, sir."

"The second one being the roar?"

"Yes, sir." Why, thought Ham, were so many questions necessary? Especially the same questions over and over.

"Could you see any large upshoot of flame forward?"

"Yes, sir; there is where I saw it first."

"Before either one?"

"Yes, sir." Ham felt like adding that he had already said so. He was not too flustered to remember that.

"But at the second explosion did you see any large up-shoot of flame?"

"No, sir. At the second explosion I was hit in the face, and I had to cover my face like this [Ham showed the members of the court] to avoid some flying pieces of iron. So I couldn't see after that."

"Was there any trembling of the ship at the first shot?"

"No, sir."

Marix had no more questions then, but Captain Sampson asked Ham if he had been looking forward at the time. Ham answered that he had been about to turn when he saw the flash.

Then Ham realized happily that the questioning was over. The tenseness left him gradually as he heard Captain Sampson's voice giving the usual instructions not to discuss matters pertaining to the inquiry outside the courtroom.

About ten minutes after Ham had risen from his chair and walked out, Apprentice Gus Dressler entered the room and was sworn by Captain Sampson.

Dressler told the court that he had been in the midship superstructure, abreast the crane locker on the port side, writing a letter. But sixty years later he was to recall that he, too, had been befuddled by the questioners. He had been on watch, not writing a letter. And to this day he regrets having forgotten in his excitement to mention to the court that he had observed a man in a boat throw something overboard near the *Maine* only a short time before the explosion.

In Havana on the same day Ham and Dressler testified, the *Vizcaya* steamed slowly into port from New York at 6:10 P.M. An excited throng lined the wharves.

Harold Martin, a correspondent for *Harper's Weekly*,

observed the arrival from the deck of a Regla-to-Havana ferry. He had heard rumors that when the *Vizcaya* reached Havana there would be trouble; Spanish feeling, bolstered by the presence of the warship, probably would explode into violence against Americans.

Martin stood on the forward deck in a crowd of Spanish officers and soldiers and wharf rabble. He watched rockets explode in the air. The smoke, he observed, drifted away in spoonfuls before the wind.

As the *Vizcaya* swung through the narrows the people broke into exultant cheers.

"*Viva España! Viva la marina de guerra!*" they shouted.

Martin heard the words. He observed that numerous rowboats and small tugs followed in the wake of the warship, like a brood of ducklings following their mother.

"Night was falling, and soon the rockets trailed tails of fire over Morro," Martin said. "Searchlights of the war vessel picked out lines of the excited mob crowded on roofs and wharves."

In view of almost everyone, even in the darkness, were the lonesome mast and twisted irons of the *Maine*.

"*Viva España!*" The shouts continued, even grew louder, it seemed to Martin. If there was to be trouble, now was the time.

The ferry on which Martin was a passenger drew close to the wreck of the *Maine*. Beyond was the *Vizcaya*, and her guns seemed mightier against the foreground of the ruined American battleship. This was a tense moment, at least for Martin, surrounded as he was by the excited Spaniards. But the danger, if there had been any, passed.

"No word against the Americans or the United States was spoken within my hearing," he said.

Lieutenant Commander Cowles, commanding officer of the U.S.S. *Fern* (aboard which Captain Sigsbee was now quartered), officially visited Captain Eulate of the *Vizcaya* after the Spanish ship had moored. Eulate then paid a visit to Cowles' ship.

He was received by Cowles and Sigsbee. But Sigsbee, having lost all his uniforms, was in civilian clothes, and the Spaniard did not immediately recognize him.

Through an interpreter, a *Fern* seaman, Eulate spoke chiefly to Cowles, until the interpreter happened to mention Sigsbee's name.

Eulate, surprised, turned to Sigsbee. The Spaniard rose from his chair, threw his arms around Sigsbee, and expressed profound sorrow over the destruction of the *Maine*.

But eight days later Sigsbee was to have reason to forget, at least temporarily, Eulate's expression of sympathy. On that day, March 9, Sigsbee moved from the *Fern* to quarters on the U.S.S. *Montgomery*. The members of the American court of inquiry had returned to Havana on the *Mangrove*, and Sigsbee and Commander George A. Converse, commanding officer of the *Montgomery*, were preparing to pay them a visit that same evening.

The gig had been called away about eight o'clock. The two men, awaiting the arrival of the boat at the gangway, were chatting in the captain's cabin when a quarter-deck messenger knocked and informed Converse that a tapping sound had been reported from a lower forward compartment.

Converse and Sigsbee rushed below to investigate. Hurrying along the main deck, Sigsbee observed that the *Montgomery* was heading to the eastward, broadside to broadside with the *Vizcaya*, which was on the port beam near the *Montgomery*.

When the officers reached the forward compartment the sound was clearly audible.

"It was a regular tapping," said the explosion-conscious Sigsbee, "like that of an electrical transmitter."

Sigsbee asked a man to time the beats. Two hundred forty a minute—"a multiple of sixty; therefore, clock-work."

No one mentioned the tragedy of the *Maine*, but it probably was on everyone's mind. At least it occupied Sigsbee's thoughts. He observed that the crew, "being forward, did not like the appearance of things."

Sigsbee suggested that a man be sent to listen to the riding cable and that someone else be sent, in a boat, to listen to the mooring buoy, to learn whether the sound was being transmitted through the water.

The tapping became louder, and the worried listeners reckoned that it must be coming from a position under a forward port compartment. Converse ordered a boat crew to probe under the port side with an oar, but the men found nothing. Then Converse abandoned all pretense of international courtesy and swept the bottom of the ship with a rope. Two boats, one on each side of the *Montgomery*, moved the submerged line from bow to stern while curious Spaniards watched from nearby ships.

"I lost my temper," Captain Sigsbee said, "and remarked that one might get as well used to blowing up as to hanging, but once was enough."

Then he and Converse realized that the sound of the tapping was slowly drawing aft, although it never ceased. Listeners reported it as most distinct at the port gangway, then in the port shaft alley abaft the gangway.

Sigsbee and Converse, on the main deck now, observed that the *Montgomery* was swinging toward the south, as was the *Vizcaya*. Both of them realized immediately that the sound had continued to be most audible in the part of the vessel nearest the Spanish warship. The noise, they concluded, must be coming through the water from the *Vizcaya*. A man sent to the forward compartment verified this. The noise there, he reported, could not be heard.

"Converse and I heroically resolved to remain on board and take our chances," Sigsbee said. The gig ordered for them returned to the boom. "We remained on board," he added, "but not heroically."

The tapping, however, finally died away, and two days passed before they had a solution to the puzzle. When Captain Eulate of the *Vizcaya* came aboard the *Montgomery* for a visit, Sigsbee and Converse laughingly told him about their recent fright.

Eulate smiled and said that the number of beats a minute indicated that the sound emanated from his dynamo or from his circulating pump.

The American court of inquiry progressed, but by now there was really no question among the public as to what the decision would be. Too much information had leaked out.

Charles Morgan, the gunner who tipped Walter Scott Meriwether about the keel, reported to the court another discovery. During one dive he had fallen into what he thought was a hole, on the port side of the *Maine*, and sunk into soft mud. Making an effort to climb back into the wreck, he grabbed the metal plates. They seemed to him to be turned inboard.

Other divers reported that the plates comprising the port side of the ship apparently had been blown inboard —or to starboard. Ensign Powelson made drawings of the wrecked hull, using information passed on to him by the divers. This helped give members of the court a clearer picture of the appearance of the bottom of the ship.

From the bow, which was sunk in the mud, the keel

angled upward until it almost reached the top of the water (as Morgan had told Meriwether) at frame eighteen. From there the keel dropped downward again to frame twenty-three, so that it formed an inverted V. This certainly suggested that a mine had been exploded under the bottom of the ship.

On the harbor floor in this area diver Thomas Smith made another discovery that gave a boost to the mine theory. He found, near the bow, a hole in the mud "four or five" feet deep. Other divers verified it.

One man said there was no such hole. William Henry Dwyer, having searched for the depression, announced that he found "no hollow such as was described." He did, however, find a spot where the ram bow of the *Maine* had scooped up "quite an amount of mud" as it turned over.

While the American court of inquiry continued its investigation, the Spanish court sought to prove that the explosion had occurred internally.

The Spaniards summoned numerous witnesses. The first one—Ensign Don Manuel Tamayo y Orellano, twenty-six, of Cadiz, officer of the deck of the *Alfonso XII* —had been questioned immediately after the explosion. He said that he sent all available boats to help the *Maine* as soon as possible.

But the rest of the questioning had not been thorough. Ensign Tamayo was not asked to tell how many explosions he heard nor to describe them. He was asked if he felt any violent quivering on board his ship at the moment of the explosion. (This would have indicated a mine detonation.) He answered that he felt nothing other than the concussion of the blast.

Another officer, twenty-two-year-old Ensign Don Guillermo Ferragut y Sbort of Palma, Majorca, had been even closer to the *Maine* when it blew up. He was in the wardroom of the transport *Legazpi*, anchored near the American ship, when the blast jarred him. He thought his own vessel had blown up, but when he rushed on deck he saw that it was the *Maine*.

The crew of the *Legazpi* also appeared on deck quickly, Ferragut said, and within five minutes all the boats that had not been destroyed by flying debris from the *Maine* were at the scene rescuing victims.

Ferragut said he did not notice any motion in the water or any vibration of his ship.

Pascual Ferrer y Juan, port pilot, had brought the *City of Washington* into the harbor about eight o'clock that evening and by nine had moored it to a buoy on the port side of the *Maine*. He said that he had been listening to a passenger playing a piano when he heard a noise "as of many rockets"—a noise like cannon reports—and then a tremendous explosion.

The Spanish court questioned numerous other witnesses, but the world awaited the decision of the United States court. On March 21, 1898, at 10:00 A.M., it came. Nobody was surprised at its conclusions.

The *Maine* had been destroyed by the explosion of a submarine mine that caused a partial explosion of "two or more" forward magazines, the court said. The evidence, however, was insufficient to place blame for the disaster on "any person or persons." The court did not give its reasons for arriving at this decision.

It was not necessary, really, to do so at the time. Most Americans were certain they knew who was responsible.

The Spanish court disagreed.

"The absence of all circumstances which necessarily accompany the explosion of a torpedo having been proved by witnesses and experts," said the report, "it can only be honestly asserted that the catastrophe was due to internal causes."

Few persons in the United States paid any attention to the Spanish decision other than to scoff at it. But the Spaniards had some telling evidence in their favor.

No witness in either the American or the Spanish court recalled observing any water thrown up by the first explosion, which would have been caused by the mine. Yet it would seem that an underwater blast would certainly cause a noticeable disturbance of the water.

Marine Private Edward McKay, who had been standing in the open on the poop deck, was asked by the American court, "Did you feel any water thrown up into the air?"

"No, sir," he answered without hesitation.

Lieutenant Blandin, who had been on the quarter-deck, also was queried about this.

"You did not notice any water as a result of the explosion?"

"None at all," Blandin said, "and none fell, to my knowledge. None fell on me, and I saw none fall around me."

Captain Teasdale, in the *Deva* half a mile away, noticed a disturbance of the water shortly after the explosion when his vessel rolled perceptibly. But First Lieutenant Don Julio Perez y Perera, testifying in the Spanish court, said that from where he stood on the shore the water appeared to be perfectly smooth. Numerous other witnesses backed him up.

More evidence, or lack of it, in favor of the Spaniards was the absence of dazed or dead fish. An underwater explosion should have left hundreds floating on the surface, it would seem, but not one witness in either court told of seeing any.

"Have you ever heard that fish leave Havana Harbor at night and go outside?" Captain Teasdale was asked in the American court.

"I have never heard any remark about that. I have seen a good many fish here, but they were small fish, just sputtering about on top of the water."

In the Spanish court Don Francisco Aldao, a diver in Havana Harbor, was asked about the presence of fish.

"They are plentiful," he answered. "Several persons earn their living by fishing inside the harbor."

Other facts favored the Spaniards.

An underwater explosion would certainly have sounded muffled, yet some witnesses described the first explosion as a sharp report.

The explosion of a mine should have tossed the *Maine* about more violently than witnesses described. None of them testified that there was a violent upheaval at the first explosion.

An underwater explosion seemingly would have transmitted through the water a perceptible shock to persons in nearby ships, but this was not substantiated by witnesses.

One fact, however, favored the Spaniards more than any other: a mine laid in Havana Harbor would have been a threat to their own shipping.

Most Americans suspected that a mine had been placed before the *Maine* reached Havana, but even Consul General Lee had been given only a few hours' notice of the battleship's arrival. After Lee had reported the impending visit to Spanish officials, they had asked for a delay. The consul general had passed this request on to the State Department, but the *Maine* arrived before Lee himself knew whether or not the request had been granted.

It seems illogical, then, that Spanish authorities would have placed a mine in the harbor, either at that time or earlier.

Perhaps a mine was planted after the arrival, some persons speculated. But the advocates of this theory evidently chose to ignore the fact that a careful watch was kept over the *Maine*. Apprentice Dressler saw someone on a boat throw something into the water near the ship, but planting a mine capable of damaging a battleship would have required considerably more effort than that.

Even supposing there had been a top-level decision by Spain to destroy the *Maine* at Havana and that somehow it had been successfully carried out, it seems extremely doubtful that the *Vizcaya* would have been ordered to visit New York.

Furthermore, it is unlikely that any responsible Spanish official could have desired a war that the sinking of the *Maine* would surely bring.

There were, of course, other possibilities. Some persons suggested that Cuban rebels caused the disaster, to bring the United States into the fighting. Many believed that a handful of Spanish fanatics rigged it. Still other theories were suggested.

But after a war had placated American hatred of the Spaniards, many persons in the United States realized that, after all, there was a possibility that the *Maine* had in some way blown herself up, that the disaster had been an unfortunate accident.

10

"*Remember the* Maine"

The war that may be upon us when these lines are read
will steady the nation and bring a calm that will be
most refreshing after the excited screaming from which
we have all suffered during the last few weeks.

—Harper's Weekly

The weeks after the sinking of the *Maine* were hectic. Few
persons in the United States doubted that war would
come, but the nation was not prepared. Government officials worked frantically to build up the armed forces. In
mid-March, Congress voted to appropriate $50,000,000
for national defense. Hurry-up orders went out for guns
and ships.

The population of the United States was estimated as
75,000,000, compared with 18,000,000 for Spain. In wealth
and natural resources the old-world nation was no match,
either, for the younger one. But Spain had an army
of half a million officers and men, including nearly 200,-

ooo in Cuba alone. On paper, at least, this far over-shadowed the 28,000-man regular army of the United States. The National Guard numbered 100,000 men, but they were poorly trained and equipped, and they had no desire for active service if it meant taking orders from a group of West Pointers.

The United States Navy was in better condition, thanks to the rehabilitation program begun several years earlier. This was fortunate for America, because it was obvious that a large part of any war with Spain would be fought on the sea. Several officials even hoped that Spain might be defeated by our navy alone, that a blockade of Cuba could do it. They were thinking, even then, only of Cuba, not foreseeing the possibility that a Spanish-American war might encompass considerably more territory.

The Assistant Secretary of the Navy, however, had a much broader outlook. On February 25—ten days after the *Maine* disaster—Secretary Long was out of the office. Theodore Roosevelt, always a man of action, sent a message to the Far East. It was addressed to Commodore George B. Dewey.

"Secret and confidential," Roosevelt stated. "Order the squadron, except *Monocacy*, to Hongkong. Keep full of coal. In the event of declaration of war Spain, your duty will be to see that the Spanish squadron does not leave the Asiatic coast, and then offensive operations in Philippine Islands. Keep *Olympia* [previously commanded to return to the United States] until further orders."

Numerous telegrams followed this, to navy command-ers around the world. Then Secretary Long returned to his office the following day and advised squadron com-manders in Honolulu, Lisbon, Hong Kong, and Key West, "Keep full of coal, the best that can be had."

A few days later the Secretary ordered that no more ammunition be expended in target practice, and on March 7 he wired Captain C. E. Clark of the battleship *Oregon*, then at Bremerton, Washington: "The situation is getting worse. You should go to San Francisco as soon as possible and get ammunition."

One month later the navy was ready. Most of the injured survivors of the battleship *Maine* had been released from the hospital at Key West; but instead of being given leaves they had been ordered to other ships.

Apprentices Ambrose Ham and Gus Dressler had been sent to the U.S.S. *Marblehead*. Seaman Mike Flynn and Apprentice Alonzo Willis went to the battleship *Iowa*. Landsman George Fox reported aboard the *Indiana*. The other officers and crew members had been scattered throughout the fleet, and wherever they went they told the story of the *Maine*. There was little doubt among them that their ship had been blown up deliberately.

Americans echoed them. "Remember the *Maine!*" was the phrase of the hour.

Richard Hovey was moved to write:

> *Ye who made war that your ships*
> *Should lay to at the beck of no nation,*
> *Make war now on murder, that slips*
> *The leash of her hounds of damnation;*
> *Ye who remembered the Alamo,*
> *Remember the* Maine!

"In a Broadway bar," wrote John K. Winkler later, "an unknown man raised his glass and solemnly said, 'Gentlemen, remember the *Maine!*' "

Millions of people picked up the phrase and flung it back at the Spanish.

Remember the *Maine!* To hell with Spain!

In Havana, the wreck of the battleship was still visible, but the night of February 15 was quickly fading into memory. After all the excitement, life in the city had returned to normal. Even the rebellion in the interior of the island seemed to be forgotten.

Havana was bustling. Business activity was off, and in the poorer sections many Cubans were starving, but the harbor and wharves were crowded with shipping. The narrow streets of the city itself were jammed with mule carts and carriages.

Harold Martin, the *Harper's Weekly* correspondent who had reported on the arrival of the *Vizcaya* several weeks earlier, described Havana at this time.

"The city is white and glistening, sun-bathed day after day in the brilliant light of the tropics. Cool breezes of the Gulf blow in from the white-capped water. Watering carts lay the dust in the streets.

"Calle General Weyler, formerly called Obispo, is shaded with awnings and gay with Spanish flags. In the shops, summer fabrics are displayed to Spanish women. Officers in tropical uniforms crowd the cafés by night."

As a Spanish city, however, Havana's days were numbered. War was coming, and even the admiral commanding the Spanish fleet in the West Indies, Pascual Cervera y Topete, foresaw a United States victory.

In early April, Consul General Lee departed. The last of the *Maine* personnel had been ordered home.

Twelve thousand miles from Havana, Commodore Dewey read a cablegram, dated April 7, from the Navy Department: "Land all woodwork, stores, etc., not needed for operations."

On that same evening the powerful battleship *Oregon* sailed from Callao, Peru, where it had been sent previously to await orders. Now Captain Clark had them: take the *Oregon*, a Pacific battleship, around Cape Horn and reinforce the North Atlantic Squadron as quickly as possible.

With no Panama Canal then available as a short cut, Clark got up steam for the long trip around the tip of South America. He enjoyed fine weather until April 16, when the *Oregon* entered the Strait of Magellan and ran into a storm.

A vicious swell made the ship pitch violently; gale-force winds screamed through the superstructure. On the bow, the jackstaff occasionally disappeared under solid seas that all but swept the topmost deck.

The storm might have sunk a less powerful ship, but the *Oregon* got through safely. With the engineers standing doubled watches for high-speed steaming (many of them even attempted to return to the fireroom after having been carried out unconscious), the *Oregon* reached Rio de Janeiro on April 30. There Captain Clark learned that war had been declared.

It had come nine days earlier. On April 19 the United States Congress had passed a resolution declaring Cuba independent. It directed the President to use force to compel Spain's withdrawal from the island.

This resolution had been telegraphed to Madrid on April 20, after President McKinley had signed it. On April 21 the United States envoy, Stewart L. Woodford, had been told by the Spanish government to leave Madrid. But not until April 25 had Congress formally declared that war existed—as of April 21.

The first shot of the war, although not really hostile, had been fired at 7:02 o'clock on the morning of April 22. The American fleet, under newly promoted Rear Admiral Sampson, had just left Florida for a blockade of the Cuban coast when a lookout on the bridge of the *New York* sighted a merchant ship loaded with lumber. The vessel displayed her flag, Spanish, and the *Nashville* was dispatched for the capture. A gunner, on signal at 7:02, fired a shot across the bow of the merchantmen, and the vessel surrendered.

She was the *Buena Ventura* ("Good Fortune") of Bilbao, bound from Pascagoula, Mississippi, to Rotterdam. Condemned as a prize, the vessel eventually became a coal barge on the American coast.

The first battle of importance, however, was to be fought far from Cuba, in an island group few Americans had heard of at that time. From the victory emerged a man who was to take a place in naval history alongside such heroes as John Paul Jones, David Farragut, and Oliver Hazard Perry.

But George Dewey almost missed the fame that the Battle of Manila Bay was to bring him. Sixty years old when the war started, Dewey had been thinking regretfully of his approaching retirement. He had spent most of his life in the navy, had been under Admiral Farragut's command during the Civil War. Several months before leaving for the Far East to assume command of the Asiatic Squadron, Dewey had visited his Montpelier, Vermont, home. There he had discussed his retirement.

"There will be no war before I retire from the navy," Dewey had told a friend, Judge Fifield, "and I will simply join the great majority of naval men, and be known in history only by consultation of the records of the Navy Department as 'George Dewey, who entered the navy at a certain date and retired as rear admiral at the age limit!' "

Now Dewey had a squadron and a war.

On April 24 the English governor of Hong Kong informed him that because of neutrality laws he must leave

the harbor within twenty-four hours. American naval officers, taking leave of their English friends at the officers' club, noted that Dewey's squadron lacked backers in
the betting on the outcome of a battle with the Spanish
fleet at Manila, under Rear Admiral Patricio Montojo y
Pasaron. No one doubted that such a battle was in the
offing.

"A fine set of fellows," the Englishmen agreed, "but un-
happily we shall never see them again."

As the first six American ships stood out of the harbor,
however, crews on English ships cheered for a Yankee
victory. The captain of one English vessel shouted as the
American ships passed, "You will surely win!"

Commodore Dewey had ordered his ships to Mirs Bay,
thirty miles from the British crown colony. The bay was
Chinese territory, and in those days China was in no position to enforce neutrality laws. The squadron had anchored there when Dewey received, via Hong Kong, instructions from Washington:

"War has commenced between the United States and
Spain. Proceed at once to the Philippine Islands. Com-
mence operations at once, particularly against the Spanish
fleet. You must capture vessels, or destroy. Use utmost en-
deavors."

The commodore delayed his departure long enough to
await the arrival from Manila of the American consul, O. F.
Williams, who could provide information for use in battle
plans.

Dewey did not have an imposing squadron under his
command. The navy had retained all its battleships in
home waters, sending to the Far East only small and comparatively weak units. The commodore's flagship was a
protected cruiser, the *Olympia*, carrying eight-inch guns
among other armament. Also in the squadron were the

cruisers *Baltimore, Boston,* and *Raleigh*—all less powerful than the *Olympia*—the gunboats *Concord* and *Petrel,* the paddle-wheeler *Monocacy,* the revenue cutter *Hugh Mc-Culloch,* the collier *Nanshan,* and the supply ship *Zafiro.* But the antiquated *Monocacy* had been left at Shanghai, and the cutter, collier, and supply ship obviously were not fit for battle.

The Spanish squadron at Manila included one more ship than Dewey had, but its largest vessel was smaller than either the *Olympia* or *Baltimore.*

Consul Williams arrived at 11:00 A.M. on April 27, and at two o'clock that same day the Asiatic Squadron weighed anchor and stood out of Mirs Bay for Manila, more than six hundred miles away. The *Olympia* led.

The afternoon was hot and still. Sailors, sweating profusely, cleared their ships for action. They unshipped and stored awning stanchions and threw unnecessary woodwork, gratings, skylights, and tables over the side.

At that moment in Manila, mustered crews of the Spanish ships were hearing a war proclamation that had been written by the governor general of the Philippines.

The American squadron crept slowly toward Manila. After sunset only taffrail lights were left burning, for each ship astern to steer by. Late in the afternoon of April 30 the vessels cut their speed and waited for darkness. The Luzon coast was in sight, and the fleet had arrived evidently unobserved.

The *Boston* and *Concord* were sent ahead to look for the Spanish fleet, reportedly in Subic Bay, a short distance north of the entrance to Manila Bay. Later the *Baltimore* was ordered to support them and to act as a linking ship for signals. Soon the word came back: no enemy ships sighted.

Dewey was delighted. The Spaniards, he concluded, were in Manila Bay.

"Now we have them," Dewey remarked to his chief of staff, B. P. Lamberton.

Admiral Montojo had indeed at first planned to engage the American squadron at Subic Bay. He reasoned, however, that the harbor there was badly protected. Like Admiral Cervera, Montojo believed an American victory inevitable, but he wanted to take advantage of every opportunity. Montojo pulled back to a position off Cavite, in Manila Bay, to take advantage of the fire cover that shore batteries might provide.

Unknown to Dewey, Montojo was notified of the presence of the United States squadron at 7:00 P.M. on April 30, but the Spaniard failed to devise a bolder plan than the one he already had.

Off the Luzon coast, Commodore Dewey called his captains to a meeting on board the *Olympia* and gave them orders for the battle. The conference was brief, and the captains quickly returned to their ships.

Between 9:40 and 9:45 P.M. the crews were called to their battle stations. They loaded the guns and waited.

Dewey's ships steamed at eight knots through the darkness toward the ten-mile-wide bay entrance. Heavy cumulus clouds, the commodore observed, had blotted out the moon.

The flagship still led. Following the *Olympia* were the *Baltimore, Raleigh, Petrel, Concord, Boston, McCulloch, Zafiro,* and *Nanshan,* with four hundred yards between ships.

Dewey, on the *Olympia* bridge, observed off the port bow the dark form of Corregidor Island, six hundred feet high at its peak. To the right of Corregidor he saw another island, Caballo, and—off the starboard bow—still another, El Fraile. The squadron was to pass into the bay between Caballo and El Fraile, which were separated by three and one half miles of water. Dewey's ships at that moment would be easy targets for the Spanish gunners.

But the *Olympia* somehow slipped through undetected. The *Baltimore* followed. By 11:30 P.M. half the ships were through before the Spaniards on El Fraile noticed glowing cinders coming from the stack of the *McCulloch* and opened fire. A shell splashed in the water between the *Raleigh* and *Petrel*.

The *McCulloch* sent three shots toward the Spaniards. El Fraile gunners fired two more times; then *Concord* and *Raleigh* batteries opened up. But from the flagship came a cease-fire order. The squadron was in now and had plenty of room. The bay was twenty-two miles long, thirty-two miles wide.

At Cavite, some Spanish naval personnel heard the shots and reported them to the admiral, who ordered his men to general quarters and ordered fires spread in all boilers. The ships were cleared for action. But defeatist Montojo still made no other change in his plan. He waited.

The long, dark line of U.S. ships steamed toward Montojo. Eight thousand miles from home, getting short on coal, and with no plentiful supply of ammunition, they were in a hostile bay. There was no way out but to fight.

The commodore ordered a slower speed, desiring not to reach Manila before daylight. He detached the *Nanshan*, *Zafiro*, and *McCulloch*, leaving them in the outer bay, and took his six warships in as a pink dawn became evident. But a low-hanging morning haze hid the Spanish fleet.

Dewey ordered the signal, "Prepare for general action," hoisted. At 5:15 A.M. a Manila battery, off the starboard bow of the *Olympia*, sent a shot toward the approaching squadron. A gun at Cavite, farther to the right, followed. Both projectiles fell far short, but the captain of the *Concord* attempted two shots at the Manila gun. After that the Americans withheld their fire. They steamed on, and suddenly they saw, toward Cavite, the Spanish fleet moored in an irregular east-west line. Nearby were the shore batteries that Admiral Montojo hoped would give his ships effective support.

Dewey ordered a column turn to starboard, to close the range on Montojo's squadron. Far ahead of the American ships two Spanish mines exploded, throwing up geysers of water and reminding some sailors of the fate of the *Maine*.

New York Herald correspondent J. L. Stickney, aboard the *Olympia*, reported on this later, possibly with a vivid imagination. The heat was intense, he said, and some men had even stripped off their shirts.

"As the *Olympia* drew nearer all was silent on board, as if the ship were empty," Stickney reported. "Suddenly, from the boatswain's mate at an after gun came a hoarse cry.

" 'Remember the *Maine!*'

"It arose from the throats of five hundred men at the guns. Their watchword was caught up in turrets and fire-rooms.

" 'Remember the *Maine!*' "

Marine Lieutenant Dion Williams of the *Baltimore* was to dispute this story later. Williams remarked in 1928:

"When we left Hong Kong the date of our latest mail was March 27. At that time the slogan, 'Remember the *Maine*,' had not yet been invented, and the warlike feelings of the crews on our ships on the Asiatic station had not run toward that revengeful sentiment. So, although it contradicts every account of the battle I have seen, in the interest of truth it should be recorded that 'Remember the *Maine*' was never shouted 'in a hoarse chorus by officers and men.' "

Ten minutes after the two mines had exploded, the Spaniards began sending a shower of projectiles in the direction of the American ships.

When the flagship was four thousand yards from the Spaniards, Dewey addressed the captain of the *Olympia:* "You may fire when you are ready, Gridley."

Immediately—at 5:41 A.M. according to the *Olympia* battle report—Captain C. B. Gridley gave the order, and a forward eight-inch gun fired. The other ships followed. All firing was to port.

When the American ships had steamed out of range, they turned and came back, raking the Spaniards this time with starboard batteries. Three more times they reversed course, gradually decreasing the range to two thousand yards.

At one time the *Reina Cristina*, Montojo's flagship, slipped the cables and attempted to ram the *Olympia,* but a fearful fire ruined the Spanish ship.

Commodore Dewey, however, was rather glum. He had not been able to discern, through the smoke, any important hits on the Spanish vessels.

At 7:35 A.M. Captain Gridley reported that there was little five-inch ammunition remaining. Dewey, amazed and disheartened, ordered a signal hoisted: "Withdraw from action." His ships steamed out of range to westward.

The Spanish fleet had been virtually destroyed.

The American gun crews were told that the ships were withdrawing for breakfast. The men, however, wanted to finish the job.

"To hell with breakfast," they shouted.

But they ate. Black coffee, bread, and meat were served

out. During the lull a report of casualties brought to light an amazing fact: not one American had been killed. Only ten had been wounded.

Dewey was informed that the report of an ammunition shortage had been an error, and the six warships returned to the attack. By this time temperatures in magazines and stokeholds had reached from 120 to as high as 160 degrees, but it failed to dim the general enthusiasm.

Admiral Montojo saw the Americans coming back.

"At 10:30 [actually it was half an hour or so later] the enemy returned," Montojo wrote afterward, "forming a circle to destroy the arsenal and the ships that remained to me, opening upon them a horrible fire."

Dewey discovered the Spanish squadron in flames. Montojo's ships put up an ineffectual resistance, and the second part of the Battle of Manila Bay was no contest. The Americans suffered no more casualties, but the Spanish total soared to 167 killed, 214 wounded. The only death in Dewey's squadron had been a man fatally overcome before the battle by the heat in one of the engine rooms.

The commodore from Montpelier had won a place in history after all, thanks—at least in part—to the *Maine*. Theodore Roosevelt—who had left his navy post to serve with the Rough Riders in Cuba—stated: "Every American is his debtor."

Congress made Dewey Admiral of the Navy and provided that he should never be retired. By his wish he was to remain on active service until his death in 1917.

But Dewey himself had little to say after the battle. In his diary this was all he wrote:

"Reached Manila at daylight. Immediately engaged the Spanish ships and batteries at Cavite. Destroyed eight of the former, including the *Reina Cristina* and *Castilla*. Anchored at noon off Manila."

11

Final Revenge

I was trying to destroy the entire Spanish fleet. That's all I was trying to do.

—Seaman Mike Flynn,
formerly of the *Maine*,
of his part in the Battle of Santiago

The war on the sea was one-sided. Not until May 11 were the first American deaths in battle recorded, and a former *Maine* officer was among them. A Spanish shell hit the U.S.S. *Winslow* off Cárdenas, Cuba, killing five persons, including Ensign Worth Bagley, a North Carolina native, who had reported aboard the *Maine* on August 22, 1897, for a brief tour of duty.

Even before Dewey's triumph at Manila Bay, the Spaniards had shown little inclination to fight. Cowardice, however, was not really the reason. The Spaniards were outmatched, and most of them realized it. They were resigned to fate.

Typical was Admiral Cervera's attitude. He arrived at Santiago de Cuba on May 19 with six warships—the *Infanta Maria Teresa*, *Vizcaya*, *Almirante Oquendo*, *Cristobal Colon*, *Pluton*, and *Furor*. The first four ships were armored cruisers, the last two destroyers. Instead of coaling and leaving at once, Cervera tarried. Scouting ships of the American fleet eventually discovered the squadron there, and Cervera's dreaded (but overrated) fleet was bottled up.

The blockading American ships were divided into two units: a West Squadron, under Commodore Winfield Schley, and an East Squadron, under Rear Admiral Sampson, who was in supreme command of both. Among the ships was the *Oregon*, which had ended her fourteen-thousand-mile dash around Cape Horn at Jupiter Inlet, Florida, May 24.

Cervera showed no inclination to come out and fight, and Sampson had no desire to risk his ships against mines and shore batteries by attempting to force his way into the harbor, which was well hidden from view by steep hills that dropped abruptly into the sea at the narrow entrance.

Sampson was willing, however, to sacrifice an old collier, the *Merrimac*, in an attempt to seal the exit on Cervera. At 3:00 A.M. on June 3, Lieutenant R. P. Hobson, in charge of an eight-man volunteer crew, took the vessel into the channel and sank her, with Spanish gunners frantically trying to beat him to it. The collier did not go down in the planned location, and the channel remained open.

By messenger Admiral Cervera informed Sampson that the crew of the *Merrimac* was safe in Santiago.

On June 22 an American army of more than fifteen thousand men landed in the vicinity of Daiquiri, east of

Santiago, and posed a new, immediate threat to Cervera's ships. The invaders met no opposition on the beaches, although Spain had nearly two hundred thousand troops in Cuba.

The army commanders had orders to march on Santiago. This would force Cervera to flee or to surrender. American correspondent Richard Harding Davis, who accompanied the invasion force, commented that this was "probably the only instance when an army was called upon to capture a fleet."

As the Americans moved inland toward Santiago, they quickly encountered furious resistance. On June 24 the first major land fighting of the campaign occurred—at Las Guásimas, a few miles east of Santiago.

In the middle of the fighting was Lieutenant Colonel Theodore Roosevelt, former Assistant Secretary of the Navy. Under Colonel Leonard Wood, he was second in command of the Rough Riders, a cavalry regiment. But Roosevelt's knack of getting his name in news columns was to bring him more fame than that received by all the other army officers combined.

Roosevelt later described the battle at Las Guásimas. "There were some minutes of the hottest of firing," he said, "before the Spaniards were driven back and slipped off through the jungle to their main lines in the rear."

The army commanders by this time had realized that they would not have such an easy time as Dewey had encountered at Manila Bay. The Spanish troops had smokeless powder, and the Americans did not. When an American fired, a telltale puff of smoke arose. Even though the American might be crouched in the dense foliage that covered most of the terrain, the smoke made a good target. Casualties began to mount.

But the Americans moved slowly forward. Then, about four o'clock on the morning of Friday, July 1, scores of buglers in the American line sounded reveille, awakening thousands of troops to a history-making day: on this day the army was to storm the heights overlooking Santiago Harbor and to defeat the Spaniards in the battles of El Caney and San Juan Hill.

It was at San Juan Hill—or, to be accurate, Kettle Hill, one rise in the San Juan group—that Theodore Roosevelt earned his reputation as a military man. Roosevelt was in immediate charge of his regiment, since Wood, newly promoted to general, commanded a brigade for this operation. Closely following Roosevelt as the Americans advanced was a newsreel photographer, Albert E. Smith, who still recalls the charge up the hill.

"Near the San Juan ford we encountered a line of regulars relaxing on the ground," he said. "When Roosevelt came up, an officer rose and saluted. 'General Shafter's compliments, sir,' the officer said. 'The general wishes that the Rough Riders will go no further.'

"Some historians quote Roosevelt as returning Shafter's compliments, then saying: 'The Rough Riders are going up the hill.'

"But I was right behind Roosevelt, and this is what he said: 'To hell with General Shafter. Come on, boys, we're going up.'"

Roosevelt himself gave a somewhat milder account of the incident, saying that he asked, "Let my men go through."

Roosevelt kept in front of the regiment as it advanced toward the top of the hill. Richard Harding Davis, nearby, observed, "The thing that impressed me the most, when our men started from cover, was that they were so few. It seemed as if someone had made a terrible mistake.

"There were a few men in advance, bunched together, and creeping up a steep, sunny hill, the top of which roared and flashed with flame."

From atop the hill, the frantic Spanish fire became fiercer as the blue-uniformed Rough Riders, ignoring casualties, crept steadily toward the summit. Then they were there, and the Spaniards retreated down the other side.

Reporter Davis said that observers at the foot of San Juan, on the American side, saw some men on top of the hill swing their hats in the air, and they heard "the sound of a tired, broken cheer."

Santiago remained in Spanish hands, but with the Americans approaching, Cervera's ships were in obvious danger. Still, the admiral made no move until he received orders the following day to flee the harbor within twelve hours.

At dawn on Sunday, July 3, the American ships lay in a semicircle around the harbor entrance, at a distance of from two to four miles from the mouth. Vigilance had been relaxed somewhat since the day before, when lookouts had spotted six columns of smoke rising from behind the hills hiding the harbor and later observed a small boat under way in the channel.

But they had seen the smoke on several earlier occasions; and when the boat in the channel disappeared into the harbor, the officers of Sampson's fleet had concluded that the signs meant nothing, after all. They had prepared for more monotonous waiting.

On the *Iowa*, however, a signalman had grabbed a halyard, bent on signal No. 250 ("The enemy's ships are escaping") for quick hoisting, and left it there.

The smoke had indeed come from Cervera's six ships, getting up steam for a dash to sea. The boat in the channel had been the *Alvarado*, removing mines.

Sunday was superb, the American sailors thought. A trifle hot, as always, but the morning was serene. There was only a slight northwest breeze, and the water was as smooth as a lake. Visibility was excellent. Many men gazed toward the island and longed to stretch their legs ashore.

The *Massachusetts* had left the line at 4:00 A.M., bound for American-held Guantánamo Bay and coal. Four and one half hours later, the *New York*, with Admiral Sampson aboard, pulled out, flying the signal, "Disregard motions of commander-in-chief." Sampson's ship was proceeding eastward toward Siboney, where the admiral was to confer with the army commander, Major General W. R. Shafter.

Left in the blockading semicircle were, from east to west, the *Indiana*, *Gloucester* (an armed yacht commanded by Lieutenant Commander Richard Wainwright, former executive officer of the *Maine*), *Oregon*, *Iowa*, *Texas*, *Brooklyn* (with Commodore Schley on board), and *Vixen* (another armed yacht). Only the *Oregon* had fires under all boilers.

Each ship faced the harbor entrance. They were like cats waiting for a mouse. They had been this way for more than a month, under orders to converge on the entrance the moment the Spanish fleet emerged.

Although the Americans were unaware of it, Cervera's squadron was under way at 9:30 A.M., when the off-watch sailors on all ships of the blockading fleet mustered for Sunday inspection. Their laundered whites glittered in the bright sunshine.

One minute later—at 9:31 A.M.—a lookout on the *Iowa*

spotted the bow of a large black ship coming into view from behind Socapa Point. Immediately he shouted an alarm, and an *Iowa* gun crew fired a warning shot. A signalman grabbed the halyard and hoisted No. 250. Captain Robley Evans bit his cigar in two as he rushed up a ladder to the bridge.

At almost that very instant, the *Oregon* fired a six-pounder, sounded its siren, and hoisted the signal.

Bugles and gongs sent the crews racing to general-quarters stations. Some men cheered as they ran.

On the *Iowa*, Seaman Mike Flynn hurried to a forward six-inch gun, and Apprentice Alonzo Willis ran to a six-inch gun aft on the port side. Both men happily contemplated the chance for revenge for the *Maine*. On the *Indiana*, George Fox rushed to his general-quarters station with the same thought.

Eight miles away, Admiral Sampson heard the guns and ordered the *New York* about, realizing the untimeliness of his Siboney trip: if the Spaniards turned westward, he would be out of the fight and Commodore Schley, an old rival, would be in the middle of it. For a few moments, however, no one except the Spaniards themselves knew which way the ships would turn. Because of shallow water, Cervera's squadron was forced to head seaward for some distance after clearing the harbor entrance.

On board the American ships, feverish activity had burst forth in the engine rooms. Getting up steam for high speed now was urgent. In the rush, *Brooklyn* engineers reportedly resorted to using salt water in boilers.

Topside, observers recognized the *Teresa*, Cervera's flagship, leading the column. At 9:40 Commodore Schley called out, "Fire steady, and give it to them." Guns of the *Brooklyn* roared. The *Texas, Iowa*, and *Indiana* also opened fire.

On the Spanish flagship, Captain Victor Concas asked Cervera's permission to fire, and it was granted. The bugler gave the signal.

Concas, facing Cervera, commented, "Poor Spain." The admiral answered, Concas said, "by an expressive motion, as though saying he had done everything to avoid it, and that his conscience was clear."

The captain of the *Teresa* later added: "My bugles were the last echo of those that history tells were sounded in the taking of Granada. It was the signal that the history of four centuries of greatness was ended, and that Spain had passed into a nation of the fourth class."

The *Teresa* opened fire, but—shooting ahead—was not able to bring a broadside to bear.

Following the *Teresa*, in plain view of the Americans now, were the *Vizcaya* (which had visited New York in February), *Colon*, *Oquendo*, *Pluton*, and *Furor*, the last ship coming into view twelve minutes after the *Teresa* had been sighted.

The Americans observed the *Teresa* swinging to starboard. Westward. Commodore Schley, on the *Brooklyn*, was in position. Sampson and the *New York* were out of it.

When the *Teresa* had completed her turn she was able to fire a port broadside, but already several of her crew had been killed, and the ship was aflame.

Still, the flagship was imposing enough to cause Commodore Schley some concern.

"Look out, Cook," he is said to have shouted to the captain of the *Brooklyn*. "They're going to ram you."

The *Brooklyn* had been steaming toward the harbor entrance, but now Captain F. A. Cook, following Schley's instructions, ordered a turn to starboard. Inadvertently still flying a signal that ordered the other vessels to follow the motions of the flagship, the *Brooklyn* steamed away from the enemy, making a complete circle before getting back on course.

Schley's flagship nearly collided with the *Texas*, which was pursuing the Spaniards. The amazed and annoyed *Texas* captain, John W. Philip, had to order full speed astern when the *Brooklyn* crossed his bow at a distance of one hundred yards—"so near," Philip commented, "that it took away our breath."

The last Spanish ships to leave Santiago Harbor, the destroyers *Furor* and *Pluton*, became quick casualties, and the former executive officer of the *Maine* received most of the credit.

Lieutenant Commander Wainwright had wisely held the small *Gloucester* back when the Spanish cruisers emerged from the harbor, but when the destroyers appeared he sped at seventeen knots to the attack, pouring shells on the hapless Spaniards.

The *Pluton* struck out for the beach at Punta Cabrera. A shell hit amidships, exploding boilers and killing all but two men in the vicinity of the engine room. The *Pluton*, by then unmanageable, plowed into the rocks and sank, only five miles from the harbor entrance.

Nearby, the shattered *Furor*, her steering gear inoperative, steamed in a senseless circle. She quickly surrendered (but later sank), and at least one person reported that the *Gloucester* men yelled exultantly, "Remember the *Maine!*" Wainwright, however, quickly dispatched his boats to rescue survivors.

One hour had passed since the *Teresa* had been sighted.

A mile and a half farther west, Cervera had ordered his blazing flagship shoreward. The *Teresa* grounded at a cove six and one half miles from the harbor entrance.

Spanish sailors lowered two boats, but both sank immediately. Those able to do so then leaped from the fiery decks into the water, several with their clothes aflame. Meanwhile, the other three Spanish warships, returning the American fire, sought to escape.

Cervera was nearly naked when he was rescued by a boat and taken to the *Gloucester*. There he was cordially received by Wainwright, who remarked that his vessel was small for so many persons. (Approximately two hundred Spaniards were aboard by then.) Wainwright promised the Spanish admiral that he would find roomier quarters as quickly as possible.

Cervera met his defeat philosophically. He had taken the ships out reluctantly, protesting to superiors that his men would certainly be slaughtered. There had never been any doubt in his mind as to the outcome of the attempt to run the American blockade.

"But," Cervera said, "I never thought our ships would be destroyed so quickly."

The *Oquendo*, last in column of the three ships fleeing westward along the coast, became the next victim. With the *Teresa* out of action, the trailing American ships concentrated their fire on the *Oquendo*, already heavily damaged, and in a matter of minutes she, too, was turned shoreward by her captain and beached—less than a mile west of the *Teresa*.

The *Colon* and *Vizcaya* raced on, but the *Vizcaya* was in trouble. Shells from the four nearest American ships— *Brooklyn*, *Oregon*, *Texas*, and *Iowa*—consistently struck her. Aboard the *Vizcaya* many shells were missing fire and several guns were jammed.

"The firing was terrific," said Captain Eulate. "Shells were bursting all around us, and the ship was on fire. My engines and pumps were disabled, and I could not fight the flames."

On the *Texas*, the jubilant crew raised a chorus of elated yells. Captain Philip admonished them, "Don't cheer, boys. The poor devils are dying."

Eulate, at 11:10 A.M., struck colors and ran his blazing ship aground at a point seventeen miles from the harbor entrance. The American vessels sped on in pursuit of the *Colon*.

By this time the *New York*, which had been far astern of the chase because of its initial handicap, had decreased the distance somewhat. Admiral Sampson signaled Captain Evans of the *Iowa* to return to his blockading station. The *Indiana* had been ordered back earlier.

In the vicinity of the *Vizcaya*, the *Iowa* stopped to pick up numerous survivors. One of them was Captain Eulate, who, upon boarding the American vessel, faced toward his ship and said, "Adios, *Vizcaya*." As if on prearranged signal, the Spanish cruiser was rocked immediately by a violent magazine explosion, and it settled deeper into the water.

The *New York*, meanwhile, had raced on in the direction of the action. Sampson's flagship had had the opportunity of firing only three four-inch shells—at the *Furor*, by that time already a shambles. Apparently, Sampson concluded, he had lost his chance; but there was still the *Colon*.

When the *New York* passed the vicinity of the wrecked cruisers, a Spaniard in the water dead ahead of the flagship called out, "*Amerigo! Amerigo! Auxilio!*"

The *New York* did not slacken its sixteen-knot speed, but Captain Chadwick altered course enough to miss the Spaniard, and a seaman tossed over the chaplain's reading desk, set up earlier for church service, for the man to cling to.

With the *Vizcaya* out of the fight, there was a momentary halt to the firing. The contest had evolved into a race only. The *Colon* had increased her lead over the *Brooklyn* to eleven thousand yards. One thousand yards on the starboard quarter of Schley's flagship was the *Oregon*. Farther back came the other American ships.

At noon the *Colon* began losing speed; the coal being used then, it developed, was inferior. The *Brooklyn* and *Oregon* closed the distance somewhat, but the Spanish cruiser was still out of effective range.

On the *Oregon*, Chief Engineer R. W. Milligan hurried up from the stokehold to the bridge. He informed Captain Clark that the coal passers below were fainting in their efforts to keep up the speed of nearly eighteen knots. If they could hear a shot now and then, Milligan suggested, they could probably live through the ordeal and keep the *Oregon* racing ahead.

Clark obliged. At 12:50 the forward turret of the *Oregon* fired. Ahead, the *Brooklyn* opened up with its eight-inch guns. None of the shells hit the *Colon*, but the Spaniards realized that their time was running short.

Observers on the American ships saw the *Colon* turn to starboard, toward land. At 1:15 P.M. a white flag went up, and the battle ended. The *Colon*, scuttled, sank at the mouth of the Tarquino River, about fifty miles from Santiago.

On the *Brooklyn*, Schley sent a message to Captain Clark.

"Congratulations on the grand victory. Thanks for splendid assistance."

On Clark's ship, it was reported, a cry went up that echoed off the rocky coast: "Remember the *Maine!*"

Ironically, the *Colon* was the only Spanish ship to surrender without putting up a stiff fight; yet she was in a much better condition to defend herself. Only one man of her crew had been killed, sixteen wounded. On the other five Spanish ships there were 322 killed, 135 wounded.

Perhaps one reason for this was that several men of the engineer force had mutinied. Unfed because of a food shortage, for twenty-four hours before the battle, they had been plied with brandy. They did well enough for a while. But when the alcoholic enthusiasm wore off, they soon tired of the action and the unbearable heat and attempted to desert their stations. United States Navy personnel who boarded the *Colon* discovered bullet-pierced bodies of several Spanish sailors in the stokehold.

Ambrose Ham and Gus Dressler, on the *Marblehead*, heard about the Santiago victory from reporters. The *Marblehead* had been anchored at Guantánamo Bay on July 3 when, at 12:45 P.M., a dispatch informed the commanding officer of the flight of the Spanish fleet.

The *Marblehead* and other ships in the bay had weighed anchor immediately and departed for Santiago, but before proceeding ten miles down the coast they had met a newspaper boat. The correspondents shouted the news across the water, and Ambrose Ham was thoroughly happy.

"Talk about crazy people!" he wrote a few hours later. "The captain, the officers, the other men, and I cheered, yelled, and jumped about the deck until we nearly had a fit."

The *Marblehead* went on to Santiago, reaching the harbor entrance after dark.

"Here we learned the details of the battle," Ham wrote. "We could see the burning wrecks, and during the night there was a terrible explosion on one of them."

Another thoroughly elated man, Commodore Schley, had quickly sent Admiral Sampson a message announcing the victory. But Sampson, having missed most of the fighting, was not in an overly festive mood. He replied with a brief request for a report of casualties.

The casualties totaled one man killed (Chief Yeoman G. H. Ellis of the *Brooklyn*, who was struck by a shell while on the bridge giving stadimeter readings) and ten wounded.

Later Schley sent his official battle report to Sampson. In it he commented, "The victory seems big enough for all of us."

Sampson evidently disagreed. In his first report to the Secretary of the Navy (which began, "The fleet offers the nation as a July 4 present . . .") the admiral failed to mention Commodore Schley or his work.

Admiral Cervera, although a prisoner after the battle, also reported to his superiors:

"The third day of July has been one of terrible disaster, as I had foreseen. Nevertheless, the number of dead is less than I had feared. The country has been defended with honor, and we have the consciousness of duty well done, but with the bitterness of knowing the losses suffered in our country's misfortune."

July 3 marked the last major battle, although fighting ashore and at sea continued until August 12. On December 10, 1898, Spain signed peace terms.

United States forces occupying Havana found that the wreck of the *Maine* was still there. Sight-seers were greatly interested in it, but naval authorities threatened boarders with a fifty-dollar fine and boatmen who transported them to the wreck with a five-dollar penalty.

The *Maine* was left alone.

12

Raising and Burial

Out of the harbor she sought long ago,
 Harbor that welcomed but served not to save,
Under the clouds, bending piteous and low
 Crept the great ship to her grave.

—Will Carleton, in
Harper's Weekly

Twelve years passed, and Americans talked about many
news events unrelated to the *Maine*. By early 1910, nine
years had gone by since the Italian engineer, Marconi,
signaled the letter *S* across the Atlantic from England to
Newfoundland; seven years had passed since Orville
Wright made his first successful flight in a heavier-than-
air craft at Kill Devil Hill, North Carolina; four years
had elapsed since the disastrous earthquake rocked San
Francisco; and it had been one year since Robert Peary
reached the North Pole.

During all that time the *Maine* had rested on the bottom of the harbor, year by year sinking a little deeper

into the mud. But one mast still poked out of the water, and around it was a pile of wreckage.

The *Maine* no longer was a household word. It was, in fact, generally forgotten, with the exception of memorial services held every February 15. Early in 1910, however, petitions to raise the ship began flooding Congress.

Most of them had been circulated by patriotic organizations, urging that the work be done to recover the remains of the dead still in the wreckage—and to examine the hull. A more practical reason given by other persons was that the sunken ship had become a menace to harbor navigation.

Later that same year Congress authorized raising the *Maine* and gave the job to the Army Corps of Engineers. Work began four months later under the immediate supervision of Major Harley B. Ferguson.

Ferguson planted an elliptical cofferdam around the *Maine*. When this was completed nine months later, the engineers pumped out the water. They retrieved the foremast and sent it to the Naval Academy at Annapolis, where it still stands, used now to display storm-warning flags. The mainmast was shipped to Arlington National Cemetery, and it stands today in the area where most of the buried sailors lie.

The entire wreck was exposed on November 2, 1911, and a second court of inquiry, under Rear Admiral Charles E. Vreeland, met eight days later to reinvestigate the cause of the disaster.

This court ruled that an exterior explosion had gone off first, but that it was not at frame eighteen—as the 1898 court had decided—but farther aft.

"The board," stated its report, "finds that the injuries to the bottom of the *Maine* . . . were caused by the explosion of a low form of explosive exterior to the ship between frames 28 and 21, strake B, port side. This resulted in igniting and exploding the contents of the six-inch reserve magazine. The more or less complete explosion of the contents of the remaining forward magazines followed. The magazine explosions resulted in the destruction of the vessel."

With the exception of the location of the explosion, the second court virtually confirmed the findings of the 1898 investigators.

Army engineers discovered the remains of an estimated sixty-four men who had gone down with the ship and never been found. Then they began making what was left of the *Maine* ready for sea—and sinking—for the last time.

They discovered that the after part of the vessel was in surprisingly good condition. The four after boilers were in place and undisturbed. They found several steam pumps in such good condition that they cleaned them and used them in the work around the wreck.

The forward part of the *Maine*, however, was so battered that the wreckage had to be cut up with torches and removed piece by piece. When this work had been completed the engineers built a bulkhead across the open end of the after part of the *Maine*, and the ship was ready to be floated.

On February 10, 1912, water was let back into the cofferdam, and the *Maine* broke away from the mud. By February 13 the cofferdam was full, and the remnant of the once-proud United States warship was afloat— two days before the fourteenth anniversary of the explosion.

One month went by; then, just after sunset on March 15, the navy tug *Osceola* towed the hulk of the *Maine* through a breach in the cofferdam, and the ship was moored to the outer wall. On the following day the *Maine* was to be towed out and sunk.

During the afternoon of that same March 15 the Havana Spanish newspaper *El Diario de la Marina* brought up an issue, quoting Chaplain Chidwick as saying that Captain Sigsbee had been ashore at a ball the night the *Maine* blew up.

Sigsbee was not in Havana for the ceremony, but Chidwick was there (to deliver a funeral oration for the men whose bodies had been found in the wreck), and he denied the story.

Nothing else marred the last rites for the *Maine*. Early the following morning a group of soldiers at Cabañas fortress fired a gun, announcing burial day for the battleship. (The gun then was fired at half-hour intervals until 2:15 P.M.)

At 9:00 A.M. the U.S.S. *Birmingham*, followed by the U.S.S. *North Carolina*, entered the harbor. The *Birmingham* fired a national salute; the gun at Cabañas answered. The two ships anchored near where the *Maine* had been moored more than fourteen years earlier.

Three hundred sailors and marines, under Commander Charles F. Hughes of the *Birmingham*, went ashore from the two ships, along with the band from the *North Carolina*, to take part in the funeral procession for the unburied dead of the *Maine*. Their remains were in thirty-four coffins at the city hall, where thirty thousand persons had filed past the day before.

Promptly at 10:00 A.M.—with the Americans formed on a street in front of the building—scores of Cuban artillerymen began entering the city hall, returning with the coffins. At 10:15 the cortege started. Twenty-five policemen headed the march. They were followed by the Havana Municipal and the *North Carolina* bands, the American sailors, and, finally, men bearing the coffins. The first one was carried by six sailors, the others by Cuban artillerymen.

At Cabelleria wharf the procession halted, and Chaplain Chidwick spoke briefly. Then United States marines transferred the coffins to launches and escorted them to the *North Carolina*.

In the early afternoon "Dynamite Johnny" O'Brien, a luminary of the Cuban revolution and then a member of the Corps of Port Pilots of Havana, went aboard the flower-covered hulk of the *Maine* with a working crew to swing the ship around, so that it would be headed in the right direction for towing.

O'Brien was to be the last pilot the *Maine* would need. He hoped to keep the hulk manageable by signaling two tugs, one hooked to each quarter of the *Maine*, to go ahead or to back engines as necessary. It would be similar to steering, by using the engines, a twin-screw vessel with a disabled rudder.

At last the working crew had the *Maine* swung right. They disembarked, leaving O'Brien alone on the vessel. He had, of course, no bridge; so he stood at the foot of a jury mast fixed in the step of the original mainmast, near the end of the after superstructure. In this part of the ship had been Captain Sigsbee's cabin.

From the masthead flew a huge American flag, "the biggest and the handsomest navy ensign I think I ever saw," O'Brien said. It had been nailed to the mast so that it would not blow away.

When O'Brien was alone on the *Maine*, and while he was waiting for the tugs to get the hulk under way, he became lost in meditation.

"I looked across that desolate deck, and there rose in my mind a picture of it bristling with cannon and crowded with strong sailormen. I never felt so much like crying in my life."

Something struck him on the cheek and roused him out of his melancholy. He saw that it was the flag, which had swung low during a lull in the breeze.

In another minute the wreck was under way. O'Brien saw by his watch that the time was 2:15 P.M. Two guns at Cabañas fortress boomed, announcing to the waiting crowd of eighty thousand persons gathered along the length of the waterfront that the *Maine* had begun her final trip. Thereafter, until the hulk was out of the harbor, a Cabañas gun fired a solemn salute every minute.

O'Brien, a black-clad figure to those who watched from the shore, observed the crews of warships standing at rigid attention as the *Maine* was towed slowly past. These ships would later fall in line behind the hulk.

Out in the channel now, O'Brien became anxious. He had no idea how the *Maine* would act under tow, and some parts of the channel were narrow even for ships under perfect control. By waving—he could not yell loudly enough—he signaled the tugs astern, while all the time the *Osceola* ahead pulled the *Maine* toward her grave.

Suddenly the tug astern to port became fouled with a projecting fragment of the wreck, and O'Brien was afraid that the tender bulkhead of the hulk would rupture and that the *Maine* would sink right there. But the tug cleared and backed off, and O'Brien saw that there was no serious damage.

Off San Telmo buoy, O'Brien knew, the channel would curve to port and become narrower. O'Brien became concerned about the danger involved in maneuvering past this area. He squeezed the ship through, however, and then he breathed more easily. He looked around.

To starboard he observed, above him, Cabañas fortress, its ramparts lined with Cuban soldiers and its saluting gun still firing every minute. Farther on he could see Morro Castle, towering over the harbor entrance, packed with spectators. To port was Havana, "whose whole population seemed to be thronging the roofs and sea walls." The men uncovered as the *Maine* went past.

Astern was the escorting fleet, with every flag at half-mast.

After a long turn to port to clear shoals under Morro, O'Brien waved off the tugs astern, and the *Osceola* paid out cable for ocean towing.

"There was a good bit of sea running," O'Brien discovered, and he thought it would be bad for the hulk.

Now, outside the harbor, the *North Carolina* fired a gun every mile. To starboard of the funeral procession the Ward Line steamer *Saratoga*, bound for New York, and the *Olivette*, bound for Tampa, slowed to allow passengers to watch the ceremony.

The *Osceola* kept the *Maine* headed into the seas, not allowing her to wallow in the trough.

"I was surprised," O'Brien commented, "to see what good weather the old hulk made of it. There was none of the quick, hard rolling that will almost throw a man off his feet."

O'Brien heard three blasts of the whistle from the *North Carolina*. This was the spot; the voyage was over. It was just outside the three-mile limit, in six hundred fathoms.

The procession halted. American warships formed to

the right, Cuban ships to the left. Other vessels took in-
termediate positions. They formed a square, more or less,
and the wreck of the *Maine* was in the center of it.

A small tug came alongside and put a working party
on board the *Maine*. On signal from the *Osceola* the
men opened sea cocks and raised sluiceways in the bulkhead; then they cast off the towline and returned to
their tug, leaving O'Brien alone again.

"I took one last look around me," O'Brien said, "to
see that nothing had been forgotten. Then I signaled
the pilot boat to come alongside, dropped into it, and
waited for the end."

Five minutes later O'Brien could see the *Maine*, with
every plunge, settling deeper forward and rising at the
stern. Aboard the warships sailors and marines stood in
close order at attention. Thousands of civilians of all
nationalities watched with bared heads.

The *Maine* gradually sank lower, although one newspaper reporter commented, "The vessel appeared to fight
against her fate. It seemed as if the *Maine* were not
going to sink."

But a few minutes later waves began washing across
her decks, and many of the flowers that had been strewn
there were now bobbing on the water near the wreck.

Twenty minutes after the *Maine* had been abandoned
she was still barely afloat. O'Brien, on the pilot boat, saw
the stern high in the air and the keel in plain view. The
ship, standing almost perpendicular to the surface of the
water, was ready to take the final plunge.

A reporter looked at his watch. The time was about
5:30 P.M. that March 16, 1912—twenty-three minutes
after the sea cocks had been opened—when the ship went
down. The jury mast struck the water flat, and the huge

ensign vanished under a sea of foam with a flash of red, white, and blue. A bugler on the *North Carolina* sounded taps.

O'Brien remembered the spectacle vividly for the rest of his life.

"Down she went, smoothly and with almost incredible velocity, her decks exploding under the pressure and hurling masses of flowers and clouds of spray into the air. In a moment she was gone.

"Then over the spot where the *Maine* had disappeared a moment before there appeared a glistening area of perfectly smooth water. In this area floated flowers; and now and then a timber or rope's end shot to the surface from the wreck."

Ships at the scene sounded their whistles in a weird sort of dirge after the *Maine* had vanished from sight; then batteries on the *North Carolina* and *Birmingham* boomed parting salutes before the two ships headed north. The *North Carolina* was to carry the coffins of the *Maine* dead to the United States for further transfer to Arlington National Cemetery.

Charles D. Sigsbee, by then an admiral, was not present for the burial of his famed ship. Neither were most other survivors, including Ambrose Ham. They probably would not have wanted to see it anyway.

But Admiral Sigsbee saw motion pictures of the ceremony, and he was greatly moved by them.

Sigsbee spoke frequently before his death in 1923 of how proud he had been of the *Maine* and of her crew, of men like Firemen First Class Karrl Christiansen, a Norwegian, who—forty-three years after surviving the explosion that blew him into the water, broke his leg, and scarred his body—appeared at a New York recruiting station to volunteer for naval service seventeen days after the Japanese attack on Pearl Harbor. Rejected for physical reasons, the sixty-nine-year-old square-jawed sailor growled as he left, "I guess the youth is only in my heart."

Admiral Sigsbee, after viewing the films, then wrote this requiem:

"The *Maine* lies in water clear and cold. I have seen motion pictures of her burial at sea. The pictured scene recurs to me now.

"She floats desolate, but flying her national ensign above the rusted hull. Again and again the waves incline her very gently. Thus she bows to fate.

"At last she pauses for a moment on her deepest incline, and then glides down to her eternal grave. A sheet of ruffled water rolls its white mantle over the spot. The waves resume their rhythm, and the material *Maine* merges into the memory of her dead."

Afterword

As the sixtieth anniversary of the explosion at Havana Harbor neared, Ambrose Ham, an alert man with a ready smile, remembered the *Maine*.

"I enjoyed my time on the ship," Ham said. It had been, after all, almost sixty years since he stood on the poop deck that night and wished for his discharge. "We had some good officers. Captain Sigsbee, for one, was most considerate. When we went into Havana Harbor he ordered awnings put up on deck for the comfort of the crew."

For hours Ham talked about his experiences on the *Maine* from the time the ship was commissioned on September 17, 1895, until the explosion destroyed her two and a half years later. He spoke, too, of four other survivors still living: Gus Dressler of New York City, Mike Flynn of Philadelphia, George Fox of Manitowoc, Wisconsin, and Alonzo Willis of Keyport, New Jersey.

Ham laughed at his narrow escape on the *Maine*. Had he not been on watch that night, or had he gone below to the engine room to brew coffee for himself and Quartermaster Harris, he, too, probably would have been killed.

Then Ham stopped chuckling. He grew solemn once more.

"You know," he said, "I don't think school children today know what the *Maine* was. The ones I talk to don't."

By simply being in Havana at the wrong time, the *Maine* earned a place in American history. Her sinking actually was the final event in a chain that led the United States to an open break with Spain. Thus, it might be said that Admiral Dewey's good fortune in moving on to fame instead of an early retirement, as he had expected shortly before the Battle of Manila Bay, was due to the misfortune of the *Maine*. If war had not come as soon as it did, Dewey might indeed have been on the retired list.

Perhaps the wrecked battleship, by hastening war, even played some part in the choice of a President. When Theodore Roosevelt resigned as Assistant Secretary of the Navy he accepted a commission as lieutenant colonel with the Rough Riders, and the man from Sagamore Hill emerged as one of the big names of the war. In 1900 he was elected Vice-President, and in 1901 he took the oath as President after McKinley had been assassinated. In 1904 Roosevelt was elected on his own.

Whatever results the sinking of the *Maine* possibly brought about, it did beyond a doubt unify Americans for the war. Although many desired a showdown with Spain even before the *Maine* exploded, there had been influential sentiment—including for a time McKinley and several of his aides—to keep the nation at peace. After the Sampson court of inquiry decision had been released, the voice of the pacifist was generally stilled.

The *Maine* also served to unify, at least temporarily, the North and the South, whose Civil War differences were still apparent.

Of greater consequence was the result of the war. The United States took over Spanish land around the globe and became a world power to be reckoned with. Isolationism was no longer practicable, although there was an attempt in that direction after World War I. United States interest in global affairs, although stimulated several years before 1898, dates largely from the months after the sinking of the *Maine*.

The war of '98 helped line up the powers for World War I. England, its long-time rivalry with Spain a factor, tended to lend moral support to the United States to an extent not given America since before the Revolution. Germany and the United States, on the other hand, developed increasing animosity. In Manila Bay at one time there was a definite threat of warfare between Dewey's ships and visiting German vessels.

There is no doubt that the sinking of the *Maine* was an important factor in the declaration of war against Spain. Whether it should have been is something else, a question argued to this day. If the *Maine* had been anchored at New Orleans, Hampton Roads, or Key West instead of at Havana, would it have exploded? It is natural to wonder how history might have been changed had this happened.

Hull plates were bent inward, United States officials pointed out as proof of an external explosion. But Fred T. Jane, writing in *Fortnightly*, asked if thin plates bent outward by an explosion within the ship might not have been bent inward later by the rush of water or by pressure.

Consider the keel, advocates of the external explosion theory advised. What else except a blast underneath the ship could have given it the inverted V shape? But an English journal, *Engineering*, suggested that the keel might have been bent when the bow sank, while the after half of the ship remained water-borne. The same writer added, however, "It may be objected that this is a somewhat bold flight to account for an upheaval of the keel thirty-four feet in such a way."

Another English journal, *Industries and Iron*, carried a letter supporting the decision of the American court of inquiry. In it an engineer stated that the explosion had been deliberate, that no column of water had been thrown up and no dead fish left in the harbor because the mine "probably was in direct contact with the ship, and the explosion relieved itself by discharging gases through the ship." Some United States Navy officers added their comments on this subject, saying: (1) the greater the depth of the mine, the less water it will throw up, and (2) many fish that float on the surface after an underwater explosion are merely dazed; later they swim away.

If a mine caused the explosion, asked the people who followed the interior theory, what became of it? No traces were found. But Commander George A. Converse, called by the first court of inquiry as an expert in explosives, said, "I have rarely seen any considerable pieces of mine. They are almost invariably ruptured and lost."

Inevitably some persons were to claim that the *Maine* had been sabotaged by some of her own crew, but this theory was so illogical that it was never taken seriously by authorities. The warrant gunner, true, was ashore that night, and he had been placed under suspension by Captain Sigsbee for disciplinary reasons. But he was never suspected by naval officials.

Inevitably, also, many accounts were to be written about the "real reason" for the *Maine* disaster. One such item, an anonymous letter sent to Consul General Lee, was appended to the record of the court of inquiry. Written in Spanish, it named persons responsible for blowing up the *Maine*, but none of the information given in the letter was verified, and members of the court paid scant attention to it.

Numerous other examples indicate that the United States court of inquiry did a creditable, impartial job of considering the evidence. One instance was the questioning of diver Carl Rundquist, who reported finding the hole in the side of the *Maine*. The metal around it, he told the court, was curved inward.

"You must be very careful," Sampson cautioned, "when you say that the edge of it was turned inboard."

Rundquist answered, "It looked to me that it was lying inboard."

"How much of it did you examine?"

"I examined parts of the edges of it. This piece I followed along in the bottom, it looked to be a good, solid piece of the ship. That must have been close to the hole where the explosion took place, because it seemed to be a good, solid piece."

"How did you think this hole was made in the bottom of the ship?"

"My opinion is, I believe that she was blown up from the outside and in, because no explosion from the inside could make a hole like that."

"Do you think there was no explosion from the inside that could make that hole?"

"There may have been an explosion from the inside afterwards, but in the first place there was an explosion from the outside."

"Why do you think so?"

"Because I would never have found the plates in the way I did."

"What strikes me is this—that you did not examine enough of that edge to form an opinion."

Although plates appeared to be turned inward and the keel was left in an inverted V, anyone who studies all the evidence in the light of history is forced to conclude that these two findings are not absolute proof of an external explosion. Too many other possibilities suggest themselves.

Perhaps Ambrose Ham had the most intelligent after-thought, one that can hardly be disputed after all these years.

On February 7, 1956, he and his wife departed for Havana. They had been given the trip by the New York State Society of St. Petersburg, Florida, where they frequently spend the winter.

When Ham reached Havana it was his first visit ashore there. Fifty-eight years earlier he had gone no farther than the *City of Washington;* then he had been evacuated on the *Olivette.*

On their tour of Havana the Hams visited the *Maine*

monument. After that they went to the waterfront. Ham pointed out to his wife the spot where the *Maine* had been berthed more than half a century earlier.

While Ham stood there, recollections of the *Maine* raced through his mind. Events he had forgotten until now. Friends and faces. Dead men. How the *Maine* had been sent to Havana, actually, to protect American citizens.

But the presence of the ship evidently brought about no change in the treatment of Americans in Havana. They had not been harmed before or after the arrival of the *Maine*, nor after the ship blew up.

Ham could not keep out a disturbing thought.

"Sending that vessel down here," he found himself reflecting, "was a mistake."

Acknowledgments

This has been an attempt to tell the story of an interesting ship, to bring together all material on it, and to place it in proper historical perspective.

For talking with me I want to thank Ambrose Ham of Binghamton, New York; Gustave J. Dressler of New York City; Michael J. Flynn of Philadelphia; and Alonzo Willis of Keyport, New Jersey —all survivors of the explosion.

Mr. Ham, who laughs when he explains that he has long since changed the spelling of his last name to Hamm, donated most of two entire days to answering questions, and he generously provided other information by mail. He lent his "log," part of which he wrote immediately after the *Maine* explosion. The last part, covering his service aboard the *Marblehead*, was written day by day at the time.

When Ham was in Havana in 1956 he told no one that he had been in the '98 explosion.

"I don't broadcast the fact that I'm a survivor of the *Maine*," he said.

In 1941 Ham retired from the postal service after a thirty-six-year career.

Mr. Dressler, a former New York City fireman who retired in 1925, also spent quite a while answering questions before a tape-recorder microphone.

"It's possible that the Spanish had no connection with the sinking," he commented. But he admitted that he and the other enlisted survivors did not believe that immediately after the explosion.

Mr. Flynn furnished much information. He denied hearing "Remember the *Maine*" shouted aboard any United States Navy ship in battle.

"But of course that's the way we felt," he added. "I was a fellow who didn't accuse anybody of anything that I didn't know was a positive fact. However, it looked bad any way you took it."

Flynn also is retired, after years of employment as a glass-plant engineer. But, unlike Ambrose Ham, he has never been back to Havana.

"I was so lucky to get away," he said, "I've never wanted to return."

Mr. Willis, after sixty years, is still emphatic in his conviction of Spanish responsibility for the *Maine* tragedy.

"A Spanish pilot took us in and to a buoy," he said, "and I think he placed us over a mine."

My thanks also go to William H. Schiela, Sr., librarian of the *Milwaukee Journal*, and to Roy Valitchka, editor of the *Manitowoc* (Wis.) *Herald-Times*, for furnishing information on another survivor, George Fox of Manitowoc.

Mr. Fox, who has a scar from an eight-stitch head injury suffered that night, is proud of active participation in three wars: as landsman—a rate (no longer used) roughly equivalent to seaman in the modern navy—during the Spanish-American War, as ammunition inspector during World War I, and as maker of gauges and special tools for submarine construction during World War II.

"I think the explosion that destroyed the *Maine* was intentional,"

Fox told a reporter in 1948, "and I'll tell you why. At 8:00 P.M. that night everything was reported secure by the gunner's mate who made regular inspections of the powder magazine temperatures.

"There were no exposed electric lights or wires that could have set off the explosion. If there had been any undue heat it would have registered on thermometers."

I am indebted to J. E. Molloy, librarian of the *Philadelphia Inquirer*, and to Margaret R. Flynn (Mr. Flynn's daughter) of Philadelphia, for sending additional information on Michael J. Flynn; to Rutherford D. Rogers, chief of the reference department of the New York Public Library, for material on Gustave J. Dressler; to the *St. Petersburg* (Fla.) *Times* and to Elizabeth Lazear of the St. Petersburg Public Library for additional information on Ambrose Ham.

Richard Krebs, a friend from West Hartford, Connecticut, talked himself into hoarseness while spending seven days in the Navy Department Library, National Archives, and Library of Congress, reading selected material into a tape recorder.

Lieutenant Commander W. H. Hunt of the U. S. Navy Office of Information (magazine and book branch) helped locate original source material on the *Maine* in Washington, D.C., as did Captain F. Kent Loomis (retired), assistant director of naval history for the Navy Department.

Isaac W. Windsor, reference librarian of the United States Naval Academy Library, prepared a bibliography of *Maine* material on hand there.

Tony Vidacovich, staff photographer of the *New Orleans Times-Picayune* and *States*, sent photostats of New Orleans newspapers published during the visit of the *Maine* in '97.

The following individuals also deserve a word of thanks:

Tom Coleman, archivist, navy branch, war records division, National Archives.

G. A. Dillinger, Kings County adjutant, United Spanish War Veterans (Department of New York), Brooklyn.

Lieutenant R. K. Hoffman, assistant curator for the Navy Department.

Richard Wesley Konter, historian, Admiral Schley Naval Squadron, U.S.W.V., Brooklyn.

Mrs. Rosalie McCann (widow of Harry McCann), Brooklyn.

Ona Lee McKeen of the Library of Congress.

Frederick Meigs, assistant librarian, Navy Department Library.

Mrs. Julia Musick, library staff, Navy Department Library.

Samuel Schaffel, commander, Admiral Schley Naval Squadron, U.S.W.V., Brooklyn.

Miss Florence Sharswood, correspondence files, naval history division, National Archives.

Carl E. Stange of the Library of Congress.

It was with great interest that I went through several newspaper files from 1898 to the present and discovered that the *Maine* has continued to make news from time to time.

At 3:30 P.M. on May 30, 1913, fifteen years after the explosion, George Hearst, son of William Randolph Hearst, pulled silken cords and uncovered a *Maine* monument in Columbus Circle, New York City. That same day, in Findlay, Ohio, Captain Sigsbee's bathtub, which had been recovered from the wreck, was displayed to thousands of curious persons.

On October 3, 1925, Arthur Rau visited Havana and for the first time since the night of the explosion saw the Cuban man who rescued him from the water.

In 1935 the United States ambassador to Spain, Claude G. Bowers, wrote President Franklin D. Roosevelt a suggestion that he obtain from Naval Academy officials an acknowledgment that Spain was not responsible for the *Maine* disaster. Roosevelt obliged, and so did academy officials. It was nothing more than a political gesture, but Spaniards expressed appreciation.

In July of 1938 a mahogany slab bearing a link of the anchor chain of the *Maine* appeared in a Jersey City furniture store window, carrying this inscription: "Compliments to the Hon. James J. Walker, Mayor of New York, from Dr. Carlos Miguel de Cespedes, Secretary of Public Works for the Republic of Cuba, February, MCMXXVII."

Informed of the find, Walker sued for return of the plaque, saying that it had been taken from his Greenwich Village home during his 1932 trip to Europe. The plaque was returned to him.

And on February 15, 1956—the fifty-eighth anniversary of the explosion—the pennant and boat ensign of the *Maine* were returned to the navy after lying forgotten for fifty-seven years in a Philadelphia attic. Maine Governor Edmund S. Muskie spoke at the ceremony, held at the officers' club of the New York Naval Ship-yard, where the *Maine* was built.

Donor of the flags was John Everetts, the gunner's mate who jumped overboard from the *Cushing* to rescue Ensign Breckin-ridge. Diver Andrew Olsen, who had probed the wreck of the *Maine* during the first court of inquiry, had retrieved the flags and had given them to Everetts, a friend, in 1898.

In preference to newspapers, magazines, and books, however, I used original source material when possible. Most of this documen-tary material—including official correspondence, battle reports, old orders, the cruise book of Naval Cadet E. H. Watson, and logs of the *Maine*—is kept in the National Archives at Washington, D.C.

If there was a conflict in published accounts, I sought to find the correct information in this material. For example, several historians differ on the order of the American ships entering Manila Bay on the night of April 30, 1898. The order I have used in this book is the order given in Commodore Dewey's battle report, a copy of which is in the National Archives.

In a few cases survivors of the explosion have told, years later, stories that do not jibe with their testimony before the court of inquiry. Unless otherwise indicated, their experiences as told to the court have been used, for obvious reasons.

Sometimes the most logical of several existing accounts was used. For example, some historians have said that signal No. 250 at Santi-ago meant, "Close in toward harbor entrance and attack enemy vessels"—logical for a flagship, but the *Iowa* was not a flagship. I chose to use the meaning, "The enemy's ships are escaping." This is the meaning given the signal in the *Iowa* battle report.

Curiosity about the subject, more than anything else, led me to compile the story of the *Maine* (which, incidentally, was redesig-nated a battleship after its commissioning as an armored cruiser). I had heard many stories about the vessel—for one, how the United States raised the ship, towed it to sea, and sank it so no one else could get a close look and see, presumably, that an internal explo-sion had occurred. I suspected that many such popular stories were based on rumor and not on fact, and this was true in many cases.

Actually, what really caused the explosion was not, and is not, known. The important facts brought out by investigations have been given; the reader may decide for himself the cause. But anyone who spends much time delving into the disaster will, I believe, conclude that there is a good chance that the ship did blow up internally, despite signs to the contrary. In any event, the explosion must have been an accident, even if an outside force caused it.

While engaged in research, I made one trip to Havana. The first day there I tried unsuccessfully to find a map showing the exact location of the *Maine* on the night it had sunk. Several persons along the waterfront gave conflicting information. Finally, I returned to the hotel.

On the veranda, comfortably tilted back in a rocking chair, sat a gray-haired man, obviously an American tourist. Thinking that the man might know exactly where in the harbor the *Maine* blew up, I began a conversation.

"Yes," he said, "I can tell you. The *Maine* blew up a thousand yards inside the entrance."

I took out a notebook and pencil.

"Happened back in 1898," he said. "The whole Spanish fleet was in Havana Harbor then. A lieutenant by the name of Hobson brought the *Maine* in and sank her, a thousand yards inside the entrance."

Later, with considerable relief, I found a map.

Bibliography

Some information was taken from each of the following sources. Whenever possible, however, original documents were relied on. The list of books does not include every volume on the Spanish-American War, but it does include most of the standard works on the naval phase of the war.

NEWSPAPERS

Binghamton (N.Y.) *Press*
Key West (Fla.) *Citizen*
Milwaukee Journal
Manitowoc (Wis.) *Herald-Times*
New Orleans Times-Picayune and *States*

NEWSPAPERS (CONT.)

New York Herald
New York Herald Tribune
New York Times
New York Tribune
New York World
Philadelphia Inquirer
St. Petersburg (Fla.) *Times*

MAGAZINE ARTICLES

(These are the most informative of numerous articles on the *Maine*.)

Akers, C. E., "The Situation in Cuba." *Harper's Weekly*, March 12, 1898.

Beehler, W. H., "Experiences of a Naval Attaché." *Century*, October, 1908.

"Burial of the *Maine*." *Outlook*, March 30, 1912.

Caldwell, J. R., "Most Mournful of Sea Pageants." [Story of "Dynamite Johnny" O'Brien] *Harper's Weekly*, May 11, 1912.

Carleton, Will, "The Funeral of the *Maine*." *Harper's Weekly*, March 30, 1912.

Cluverius, W. T., "A Midshipman on the *Maine*." U. S. Naval Institute *Proceedings*, February, 1918.

Davis, Richard Harding, "The Battle of San Juan." *Scribner's*, October, 1898.

[Editorial] *Harper's Weekly*, March 19 and April 23, 1898.

"Foreign Expert Opinion on the *Maine* Disaster." *Scientific American*, May 21, 1898.

Jane, F. T., "*Maine* Disaster and After." *Fortnightly*, April, 1898.

Johnson, Arthur M., "The Battleship *Maine* and Pier 46, East River." U. S. Naval Institute *Proceedings*, November, 1955.

"Last of the *Maine:* A Fitting Burial at Sea." *Scientific American*, March 30, 1912.

"Launch of the Armored Cruiser *Maine* at the Brooklyn Navy Yard." *Scientific American*, November 29, 1890.

Leupp, F. E., "The Disaster to the Battle-ship 'Maine.'" *Harper's Weekly*, February 26, 1898.

Leupp, F. E., "*Maine* Report." *Harper's Weekly*, April 2, 1898.

Martin, Harold [Report from Havana] *Harper's Weekly*, March 12, March 19, March 26, 1898.

Melville, George W., "The Destruction of the *Maine*." *North American Review*, June, 1911.

Meriwether, Walter Scott, "Remembering the *Maine*." U. S. Naval Institute *Proceedings*, May, 1948.

Meriwether, Walter Scott, "Unremembered *Maine*." *Harper's Weekly*, July 11, 1908.

Rea, George Bronson, "The Night of the Explosion in Havana." *Harper's Weekly*, March 5, 1898.

Roosevelt, Theodore, "The Rough Riders." *Scribner's*, January-April, 1899.

Scientific American, April 8, 1898.

Sigsbee, Charles D., "My Story of the 'Maine.'" *Cosmopolitan*, July, August, 1912.

"Situation at Key West." *Harper's Weekly*, March 5, 1898.

BOOKS

Annual Reports of the Navy Department, 1898. Washington, D.C.: Government Printing Office, 1898.

Chadwick, French E., *The Relations of the United States and Spain—The Spanish-American War*. New York: Scribner's, 1911 (2v).

Chidwick, John P., *Remember the* Maine. Winchester, Va.: Winchester Printers and Stationers [n.d.].

Dewey, George, *Autobiography of George Dewey*. New York: Scribner's, 1913.

Encyclopedia Americana. New York: Americana Corporation, 1954.

Evans, Robley D., *A Sailor's Log*. New York: Appleton, 1901.

Grieg, Julius, *The Immediate Cause of the War with Spain*. [n.p., n.d.] (This purports to bare the facts of a plot against the *Maine* but is of value only as a curiosity. The Library of Congress has a copy, the Navy Department Library a photostat.)

Hammond's Complete World Atlas. New York: C. S. Hammond, 1950.

Kane, Joseph Nathan, *Famous First Facts*. New York: H. W. Wilson, 1950.

BOOKS (CONT.)

Lodge, Henry Cabot, *The War with Spain*. New York: Harper, 1900.

Mason, Gregory, *Remember the Maine*. New York: Holt, 1939.

Millis, Walter, *The Martial Spirit*. Boston: Houghton Mifflin, 1931.

Mitchell, D. W., *History of the Modern American Navy*. New York: Knopf, 1946.

Pictorial Atlas Illustrating the Spanish-American War. [n.p.] Souvenir Publishing Company, 1899.

Report of the Naval Court of Inquiry Upon the Destruction of the United States Battle Ship Maine. [Senate Document No. 207, 55th Congress, 2d Session.] Washington, D.C.: Government Printing Office, 1898.

Report of the Spanish Naval Board of Inquiry as to the Cause of the Destruction of the U.S.B.S. Maine. [Reprinted in Senate Report No. 885, 55th Congress, 2d Session.] Washington, D.C.: Government Printing Office, 1898.

Schley, Winfield S., *Forty-Five Years under the Flag*. New York: Appleton, 1904.

Sigsbee, Charles D., *The 'Maine.'* New York: Century, 1899.

Spears, John R., *A History of the United States Navy*. New York: Scribner's, 1908.

Smith, Albert E., *Two Reels and a Crank*. Garden City: Doubleday, 1952. (In collaboration with Phil A. Koury.)

West, Richard S., Jr., *Admirals of American Empire*. Indianapolis: Bobbs-Merrill, 1948.

Wilson, H. W., *The Downfall of Spain*. Boston: Little, Brown, 1900.

Winkler, John K., *W. R. Hearst*. New York: Simon and Schuster, 1928.

List of Officers and Crew

Twenty-six officers made up the ship's company of the *Maine* at the time of the explosion. Existing Navy Department records do not list home towns for all of them.

Captain Charles D. Sigsbee, commanding officer
Lieutenant Commander Richard Wainwright, executive officer
Lieutenant George F. W. Holman
Lieutenant John Hood
Lieutenant Carl W. Jungen
Lieutenant Junior Grade George P. Blow
Lieutenant Junior Grade John J. Blandin
Lieutenant Junior Grade Friend W. Jenkins
Naval Cadet Jonas H. Holden

Naval Cadet W. T. Cluverius
Naval Cadet Amon Bronson, Jr.
Naval Cadet David F. Boyd, Jr.
Surgeon Lucien G. Heneberger
Paymaster Charles M. Ray
Chief Engineer Charles P. Howell
Passed Assistant Engineer Frederic C. Bowers
Assistant Engineer John R. Morris
Assistant Engineer Darwin R. Merritt
Naval Cadet (engineer) Pope Washington
Naval Cadet (engineer) Arthur Crenshaw
Chaplain John P. Chidwick
First Lieutenant Albertus W. Catlin, U.S.M.C.
Boatswain Francis E. Larkin
Gunner Joseph Hill
Carpenter George Helms
Pay Clerk Brent McCarthy

Two officers, Jenkins (of Allegheny City, Pa.) and Merritt (of Red Oaks, Ia.), died in the explosion. Another, Blandin (of Baltimore, Md.), died several months later. Four officers—Bowers, Washington, McCarthy, and Hill—were not aboard when the ship blew up.

The following list of the crew, all of whom were aboard, shows 250 as missing or dead and eight as having died within the next few days. With the two deaths among the officers, this gives a total of 260. Other accounts, probably taking into consideration subsequent deaths that could be blamed on the explosion, list 266 fatalities.

NAME AND RATE	HOME	FATE
Adams, John T., Coal Passer	Washington, D.C.	Missing
Aitken, James P., Boatswain's Mate First Class	Norfolk, Va.	Missing
Allen, James W., Mess Attendant	Norfolk, Va.	Injured
Andersen, Holm A., Coal Passer	Christiana, Norway	Missing
Anderson, Axel C., Seaman	Copenhagen, Denmark	Missing
Anderson, Charles, Landsman	Norfolk, Va.	Missing
Anderson, Gustav A., Seaman	Uddevalla, Sweden	Missing

NAME AND RATE	HOME	FATE
Anderson, John, Boatswain's Mate Second Class	New York City	Dead
Anderson, John, Seaman	Tonsberg, Norway	Missing
Anderson, Oskar, Coxswain	Söderhamn, Sweden	Injured
Andrews, Frank, Ordinary Seaman	Chemung, N.Y.	Dead
Anthony, William, Private	Albany, N.Y.	Uninjured
Auchenbach, Harry, Fireman Second Class	Newmanstown, Pa.	Missing
Aufindsen, Abraham, Coxswain	Stavanger, Norway	Missing
Augland, Bernhard, Blacksmith	Östersund, Sweden	Missing
Awo, Firsanion, Steerage Cook	Mikawa, Japan	Injured
Barry, John P., Apprentice First Class	not listed	Dead
Barry, Lewis L., Coal Passer	Halifax, N.S.	Missing
Baum, Henry S., Landsman	New York City	Missing
Becker, Jakob, Chief Machinist	Hoboken, N.J.	Missing
Bell, John R., Cabin Steward	not listed	Missing
Bennet, John, Private	New York City	Dead
Bergman, Charles, Boatswain's Mate First Class	Västervik, Sweden	Injured
Blomberg, Fred, Landsman	Chicago, Ill.	Missing
Bloomer, John H., Landsman	East Deering, Me.	Injured
Boll, Fritz, Bayman	Berlin, Germany	Dead
Bonner, Leon, Seaman	New York City	Missing
Bookbinder, John, Apprentice Second Class	Brooklyn, N.Y.	Missing
Botting, Vincent H., Private	New York City	Missing
Boyle, James, Quartermaster First Class	New York City	Dead
Brinkman, Henrich, Seaman	Tompkinsville, N.Y.	Missing
Brofeldt, Arthur, Chief Gunner's Mate	Helsingfors, Finland	Missing
Brosnan, George, Private	Brooklyn, N.Y.	Missing
Brown, James T., Sergeant	Buncrana, Ireland	Dead
Bruns, Adolph C., Quartermaster Third Class	Baltimore, Md.	Missing
Bullock, Charles H., Gunner's Mate Second Class	Newburgh, N.Y.	Uninjured

NAME AND RATE	HOME	FATE
Burkhardt, Robert, Quartermaster Second Class	Hamburg, Germany	Dead
Burns, Edward, Coal Passer	Charlestown, Mass.	Missing
Burns, James R., Corporal	Brooklyn, N.Y.	Missing
Butler, Frederick F., Machinist Second Class	Harrison, N.J.	Missing
Cahill, Francis D., Landsman	Salem, Mass.	Injured
Caine, Thomas, Blacksmith	Portsmouth, Va.	Missing
Cameron, Walter, Seaman	Providence, R.I.	Missing
Carr, Herbert M., Gunner's Mate Second Class	Camden, N.J.	Missing
Caulfield, William, Landsman	New Orleans, La.	Missing
Chingi, Suke, Mess Attendant	not listed	Missing
Christiansen, Carl A., Fireman First Class	Brooklyn, N.Y.	Missing
Christiansen, Karrl, Fireman First Class	Stavanger, Norway	Injured
Clark, Thomas, Coal Passer	Newark, N.J.	Missing
Clarke, James C., Shipwright	New York City	Missing
Cochrane, Michael, Fireman First Class	Fall River, Mass.	Missing
Coffey, John, Private	Somerville, Mass.	Injured
Cole, Thomas M., Bayman	Philadelphia, Pa.	Dead
Coleman, William, Ordinary Seaman	New York City	Missing
Coleman, William, Fireman Second Class	Brooklyn, N.Y.	Missing
Conroy, Anthony, Coal Passer	Galway, Ireland	Dead
Cosgrove, William, Fireman Second Class	not listed	Dead
Cronin, Daniel, Landsman	New York City	Injured
Curran, Charles, Coxswain	County Donegal, Ireland	Dead
Dahlman, Berger, Seaman	Oskarshamn, Sweden	Missing
David, George, Ordinary Seaman	Malta	Injured
Dennig, Charles, Seaman	Newark, N.J.	Missing
Dierking, John H., Drummer	Brooklyn, N.Y.	Dead
Dolan, John, Seaman	Brookline, Mass.	Uninjured

NAME AND RATE	HOME	FATE
Donoughy, William, Ordinary Seaman	Londonderry, Ireland	Dead
Downing, Michael J., Private	South Boston, Mass.	Missing
Dressler, Gustave J., Apprentice First Class	New York City	Injured
Drury, James, Fireman First Class	Brooklyn, N.Y.	Missing
Durckin, Thomas J., Ordinary Seaman	Salem, Mass.	Injured
Edler, George, Seaman	not listed	Missing
Eiermann, Charles, Gunner's Mate First Class	Eberbach, Germany	Dead
Erikson, Andrew V., Seaman	Union Hill, N.J.	Died later
Etts, John P., Seaman	Rochester, N.Y.	Missing
Evensen, Carl, Seaman	Brooklyn, N.Y.	Missing
Fadde, Charles, Apprentice First Class	Elizabeth, N.J.	Missing
Falk, Rudolph, Oiler	New York City	Missing
Faubel, George D., Chief Machinist	Baltimore, Md.	Missing
Fewer, William, Boatswain's Mate Second Class	Providence, R.I.	Dead
Finch, Trubie, Apprentice First Class	Raleigh, N.C.	Dead
Fisher, Alfred J., Oiler	Newport, England	Missing
Fisher, Frank, Ordinary Seaman	Detroit, Mich.	Died later
Flaherty, Michael, Fireman First Class	Portsmouth, Va.	Missing
Fleishman, Lewis M., Seaman	Baltimore, Md.	Missing
Flynn, Michael, Seaman First Class	Philadelphia, Pa.	Injured
Flynn, Patrick, Fireman Second Class	County Waterford, Ireland	Dead
Foley, Patrick J., Apprentice First Class	Orange, N.J.	Injured
Fougere, John, Coal Passer	Arichat, Cape Breton	Missing
Fountain, Bartley, Boatswain's Mate First Class	Quebec, Canada	Missing

NAME AND RATE	HOME	FATE
Fox, George, Landsman	Manitowoc, Wis.	Injured
Franke, Charles, Apprentice First Class	Brooklyn, N.Y.	Missing
Furlong, James F., Coal Passer	South Cleveland, Ohio	Missing
Gaffney, Patrick, Fireman First Class	County Roscommon, Ireland	Dead
Galpin, C. P., Private	Falls Church, Va.	Uninjured
Gardner, Frank, Coal Passer	New York City	Missing
Gardner, Thomas J., Chief Yeoman	Brooklyn, N.Y.	Missing
Gartrell, William, Fireman First Class	Washington, D.C.	Uninjured
Germond, Chester V., Private	Poughkeepsie, N.Y.	Injured
Gordon, Joseph F., Fireman First Class	Portsmouth, Va.	Dead
Gorman, William, Ordinary Seaman	Boston, Mass.	Missing
Grady, Patrick, Coal Passer	County Kildare, Ireland	Missing
Graham, Edward P., Coal Passer	Jersey City, N.J.	Missing
Graham, James A., Chief Yeoman	Newport, R.I.	Dead
Greer, William A., Apprentice First Class	Brooklyn, N.Y.	Missing
Griffin, Michael, Fireman Second Class	Dublin, Ireland	Missing
Gross, Henry, Landsman	New York City	Dead
Grupp, Reinhardt, Coal Passer	Chicago, Ill.	Missing
Hallberg, Alfred, Coxswain	Oroust, Iceland	Injured
Hallberg, John A., Oiler	Sweden	Missing
Ham, Ambrose, Apprentice First Class	Schenectady, N.Y.	Injured
Hamberger, William, Landsman	Jersey City, N.J.	Missing
Hamilton, Charles A., Apprentice First Class	Newport, R.I.	Missing
Hamilton, John, Chief Carpenter's Mate	Brooklyn, N.Y.	Missing

NAME AND RATE	HOME	FATE
Hanrahan, William C., Coxswain	Cohoes, N.Y.	Missing
Harley, Daniel O., Fireman Second Class	Philadelphia, Pa.	Missing
Harris, Edward, Water Tender	Binghamton, N.Y.	Missing
Harris, Millard F., Quartermaster Third Class	Boothbay Harbor, Me.	Dead
Harris, Westmore, Mess Attendant	Charles City, Va.	Uninjured
Harty, Thomas J., Coal Passer	New York City	Dead
Hassel, Charles, Gunner's Mate Third Class	Saba, W.I.	Dead
Hauck, Charles, Landsman	Brooklyn, N.Y.	Missing
Hawkins, Howard B., Ordinary Seaman	West Bay City, Mich.	Missing
Heffron, John, Ordinary Seaman	Brooklyn, N.Y.	Injured
Hennekes, Albert B., Gunner's Mate Second Class	Cincinnati, Ohio	Dead
Herbert, John, Landsman	Brooklyn, N.Y.	Injured
Herness, Alfred B., Gunner's Mate Third Class	Trondheim, Norway	Injured
Herriman, Benjamin H., Apprentice First Class	Chaptico, Md.	Missing
Holland, Alfred J., Coxswain	South Brooklyn, N.Y.	Died later
Holm, Gustav, Boatswain's Mate Second Class	Horten, Norway	Dead
Holzer, Frederick C., Ordinary Seaman	Brooklyn, N.Y.	Died later
Horn, William, Fireman First Class	Whitehall, N.Y.	Dead
Hough, William, Landsman	New York City	Missing
Hughes, Patrick, Fireman First Class	King's County, Ireland	Dead
Hutchings, Robert, Landsman	New York City	Injured
Ishida, Otogira, Steerage Cook	Yokohama, Japan	Missing
Jectson, Harry, Seaman	Los Angeles, Calif.	Died later
Jencks, Carlton, Gunner's Mate Third Class	La Salle County, Ill.	Dead

NAME AND RATE	HOME	FATE
Jernee, Fred, Coal Passer	Brooklyn, N.Y.	Died later
Johansen, Peter C., Seaman	Denmark	Missing
Johnson, Alfred, Seaman	Stockholm, Sweden	Injured
Johnson, Charles, Ordinary Seaman	Lynn, Mass.	Missing
Johnson, Charles Ehler, Private	Lancaster, Pa.	Missing
Johnson, George, Coal Passer	Washington, D.C.	Dead
Johnson, John W., Landsman	not listed	Dead
Johnsson, Peter, Oiler	Sweden	Missing
Jones, Thomas, Coal Passer	Ottawa, Ill.	Dead
Jordan, William Joseph, Private	Tilton, N.H.	Missing
Just, Charles, Apprentice First Class	Charleston, S.C.	Dead
Kane, Joseph H., Landsman	Worcester, Mass.	Injured
Kane, Michael, Coal Passer	County Galway, Ireland	Missing
Kay, John A., Machinist First Class	Rising Star, Md.	Missing
Kean, Edward F., Private	Chicago, Ill.	Missing
Kelly, Frank, Private	South Boston, Mass.	Missing
Kelly, Hugh, Coal Passer	Brooklyn, N.Y.	Missing
Kelly, John, Coal Passer	Brooklyn, N.Y.	Missing
Kesskull, Alexander, Seaman	Stettin, Germany	Missing
Keys, Harry, Ordinary Seaman	Hartine, Wash.	Dead
Kihlstrom, Fritz, Ordinary Seaman	Sweden	Missing
Kinsella, Thomas, Machinist Second Class	Washington, D.C.	Missing
Kinsey, Frederick, Machinist Second Class	Newark, N.J.	Missing
Kitogata, Yukishi, Warrant Officers' Cook	Kobe, Japan	Missing
Kniese, Frederick, Machinist First Class	Memphis, Tenn.	Dead
Koebler, George, Apprentice First Class	Brooklyn, N.Y.	Died later
Kranyak, Charles, Apprentice First Class	England	Missing

NAME AND RATE	HOME	FATE
Kruse, Hugo, Painter	Long Island, N.Y.	Missing
Kushida, Katsusaburo, Warrant Officers' Steward	Hiroshima, Japan	Uninjured
Laird, Charles, Master-at-Arms Third Class	Everett, Mass.	Missing
Lambert, William, Fireman Second Class	Hampton, Va.	Missing
Lanahan, Michael, Landsman	Louisville, Ky.	Injured
Lancaster, Luther, Boatswain's Mate Second Class	Fredericksburg, Va.	Missing
Lapierre, George, Apprentice First Class	Montreal, Canada	Missing
Larsen, Peder, Seaman	Brooklyn, N.Y.	Uninjured
Lauriette, George, Private	Lowell, Mass.	Missing
Lawler, Edward, Coal Passer	Liverpool, England	Missing
League, James, Chief Yeoman	Annapolis, Md.	Dead
Lee, William, Apprentice First Class	Ramsey, N.J.	Missing
Leene, Daniel, Coal Passer	Ansonia, Conn.	Missing
Lees, Samuel, Ordinary Seaman	New York City	Dead
Leupold, Gustav, Fireman Second Class	Newark, N.J.	Missing
Lewis, Daniel, Oiler	Washington, D.C.	Missing
Lewis, John B., Water Tender	Baltimore, Md.	Missing
Lieber, George, Apprentice First Class	New York City	Missing
Load, John B., Master-at-Arms Third Class	London, England	Uninjured
Loftus, Paul, Private	Scranton, Pa.	Injured
Lohman, Charles, Coal Passer	Uppsala, Sweden	Injured
Lorenzen, Jorgen, Oiler	Sönderborg, Germany	Missing
Losko, Peter, Private	Brooklyn, N.Y.	Missing
Louden, James, Apprentice	Keyport, N.J.	Dead
Lowell, Clarence, Ordinary Seaman	South Gardiner, Me.	Missing
Lund, William, Coxswain	Finland	Missing
Lutz, Joseph, Private	Passaic, N.J.	Uninjured
Lydon, John T., Ordinary Seaman	New York City	Missing

NAME AND RATE	HOME	FATE
Lynch, Bernard, Fireman First Class	Portland, Me.	Missing
Lynch, Matthew, Coal Passer	Providence, R.I.	Missing
McCann, Harry, Seaman	Vallejo, Calif.	Injured
McGonigle, Hugh, Fireman Second Class	County Donegal, Ireland	Missing
Mack, Thomas, Landsman	Baltimore, Md.	Injured
McDermott, John, Private	New York City	Missing
McDevitt, William, Private	Listowel, Ireland	Injured
McGuinness, William, Private	County Tyrone, Ireland	Injured
McKay, Edward, Private	Hartford, Conn.	Uninjured
McManus, John, Fireman Second Class	Davenport, Ia.	Dead
McNair, William, Ordinary Seaman	Pittsburgh, Pa.	Injured
McNiece, Francis, Coal Passer	Charlestown, Mass.	Dead
Magamine, Tomekishi, Mess Attendant	Japan	Missing
Malone, Michael, Fireman Second Class	New York City	Missing
Marsden, Benjamin, Apprentice First Class	Jersey City, N.J.	Missing
Marshall, John, Landsman	Cincinnati, Ohio	Missing
Martensson, Johan, Gunner's Mate Third Class	Copenhagen, Denmark	Missing
Mason, James H., Landsman	Jersey City, N.J.	Missing
Matiasen, Carl, Seaman	Philadelphia, Pa.	Missing
Mattisen, William, Ordinary Seaman	West Bay City, Mich.	Injured
Matssen, Edward, Ordinary Seaman	Skillinge, Sweden	Injured
Matza, John, Coal Passer	East Saint Louis, Ill.	Dead
Meehan, Michael, Sergeant	County Sligo, Ireland	Uninjured
Meilstrup, Elmer, Ordinary Seaman	West Bay City, Mich.	Missing
Melville, Thomas, Coal Passer	New York City	Uninjured
Mero, Eldon, Chief Machinist	Philadelphia, Pa.	Dead
Merz, John, Landsman	Brooklyn, N.Y.	Missing

NAME AND RATE	HOME	FATE
Mikkelsen, Peter, Seaman	Abeltoft, Denmark	Injured
Miller, George, Seaman	New York City	Missing
Miller, William, Apprentice Second Class	New York City	Missing
Mobles, George, Coxswain	Cephalonia, Greece	Missing
Monahan, Joseph, Private	Roxbury, Mass.	Missing
Monfort, William, Landsman	Council Bluffs, Ia.	Missing
Moore, Edward, Coal Passer	Charles City, Va.	Missing
Morinière, Louis, Seaman	Le Havre, France	Injured
Moss, Gerhard, Machinist First Class	Brooklyn, N.Y.	Missing
Moss, John H., Landsman	Rainwood, N.C.	Missing
Mudd, Noble T., Seaman	Washington, D.C.	Dead
Murphy, Cornelius, Oiler	County Cork, Ireland	Missing
Newman, F. J., Private	New York City	Missing
Newton, C. H., Fifer	Washington, D.C.	Missing
Nielsen, John C., Seaman	Copenhagen, Denmark	Missing
Nielsen, Sophus, Coxswain	Odense, Denmark	Dead
Noble, William, Fireman Second Class	New York City	Missing
Nolan, Charles, Gunner's Mate Third Class	Boston, Mass.	Missing
O'Connor, James, Chief Boatswain's Mate	Bayonne, N.J.	Missing
O'Hagan, Thomas, Apprentice First Class	New York City	Missing
Ohye, Mas, Mess Attendant	Japan	Missing
O'Neill, Patrick, Fireman Second Class	County Louth, Ireland	Missing
Ording, Gustav, Carpenter's Mate Third Class	Newport, Ky.	Missing
O'Regan, Henry, Water Tender	East Boston, Mass.	Missing
Paige, Frederick, Landsman	Buffalo, N.Y.	Missing
Palmgren, John, Seaman	Helsingborg, Sweden	Missing
Panck, John, Fireman First Class	Lynchburg, Va.	Injured
Perry, Robert, Mess Attendant	Norfolk, Va.	Missing

NAME AND RATE	HOME	FATE
Phillips, Francis, Apprentice First Class	Rochester, N.Y.	Dead
Pilcher, Charles, Ordinary Seaman	Detroit, Mich.	Injured
Pinkney, James, Mess Attendant	Norfolk, Va.	Dead
Porter, John, Coal Passer	Tom's Ridge, N.Y.	Missing
Powers, John, Oiler	County Cork, Ireland	Missing
Price, Daniel, Fireman First Class	Stoneham, Mass.	Dead
Quigley, Thomas, Plumber and Fitter	New York City	Missing
Quinn, Charles, Oiler	Boston, Mass.	Missing
Rau, Arthur, Seaman	Stettin, Germany	Injured
Reden, Martin, Seaman	Union Hill, N.J.	Uninjured
Reilly, Joseph, Fireman First Class	New York City	Missing
Richards, Walter, Apprentice Second Class	Westville, N.J.	Injured
Richter, A. H., Corporal	Chicago, Ill.	Missing
Rieger, William, Gunner's Mate First Class	Washington, D.C.	Missing
Rising, Newell, Coal Passer	Portchester, N.J.	Missing
Roberts, James, Private	Randolph, Mass.	Dead
Robinson, William, Landsman	Hoboken, N.J.	Missing
Roos, Peter, Sailmaker	Christianstad, Sweden	Missing
Rowe, James, Ship's Cook Fourth Class	Tottenham, England	Injured
Rusch, Frank, Ordinary Seaman	Detroit, Mich.	Injured
Rushworth, William, Chief Machinist	Norfolk, Va.	Dead
Safford, Clarence, Gunner's Mate First Class	Taunton, Mass.	Missing
Salmin, Michael, Ordinary Seaman	Russia	Missing
Schoen, Joseph, Corporal	New York City	Dead
Schroeder, August, Ordinary Seaman	Brooklyn, N.Y.	Missing

NAME AND RATE	HOME	FATE
Schwartz, George, Ship's Cook First Class	Hanover, Germany	Injured
Scott, Charles, Carpenter's Mate Second Class	Freeport, N.Y.	Dead
Scully, Joseph, Boilermaker	Baltimore, Md.	Dead
Seery, Joseph, Fireman First Class	County Kildare, Ireland	Dead
Sellers, Walter, Apothecary	Shelby, Ohio	Dead
Shea, Jeremiah, Coal Passer	Haverhill, Mass.	Injured
Shea, John, Coal Passer	New York City	Missing
Shea, Patrick, Firemen First Class	Willimantic, Conn.	Missing
Shea, Thomas, Landsman	New York City	Missing
Sheridan, Owen, Fireman Second Class	County Cavan, Ireland	Dead
Shillington, John, Yeoman Third Class	Chicago, Ill.	Missing
Simmons, Alfred, Coal Passer	Portsmouth, Va.	Dead
Smith, Carl, Seaman	Hamburg, Germany	Died later
Smith, Nicholas, Apprentice First Class	Lynchburg, Va.	Dead
Stevenson, Nicholas, Seaman	Christiansand, Norway	Missing
Stock, H. E., Private	New York City	Missing
Strongman, James, Private	Prince Edward Island	Missing
Sugisaki, Isa, Wardroom Steward	Muro Odawara Kaoagawa, Japan	Missing
Suman, E. B., Private	Hagerstown, Md.	Dead
Sutton, Frank, Fireman Second Class	Galveston, Tex.	Dead
Suzuki, Kashotora, Mess Attendant	Japan	Dead
Talbot, Frank, Landsman	Bath, Me.	Missing
Teackle, Harry, Seaman	St. George, N.Y.	Injured
Tehan, Daniel, Coal Passer	New York City	Missing
Thompson, George, Landsman	Ionian Islands, Greece	Missing
Thompson, F. G., Corporal	Charlestown, Mass.	Injured
Thompson, William, Landsman	New York City	Injured

NAME AND RATE	HOME	FATE
Tigges, Frank, Coppersmith	Oelde, Germany	Dead
Timpany, E. B., Private	Digby, Nova Scotia	Missing
Tinsman, William, Landsman	East Deering, Me.	Dead
Todoresco, Constantin, Fireman	Brăila, Romania	Missing
Toppin, Daniel, Wardroom Cook	New York City	Injured
Troy, Thomas, Coal Passer	Waterbury, Conn.	Missing
Tuohey, Martin, Coal Passer	Brooklyn, N.Y.	Missing
Turpin, John, Mess Attendant	Long Branch, N.Y.	Uninjured
Van Horn, H. A., Private	Philadelphia, Pa.	Missing
Wagner, Henry, First Sergeant	Dürkheim, Germany	Dead
Wallace, John, Ordinary Seaman	South Boston, Mass.	Missing
Walsh, Joseph, Coxswain	Brockton, Mass.	Missing
Warren, Asa, Private	Craven County, N.C.	Missing
Warren, John, Fireman Second Class	Randolph, S.C.	Missing
Waters, Thomas, Landsman	Philadelphia, Pa.	Injured
Webber, Martin, Landsman	Bar Harbor, Me.	Injured
White, Charles, Chief Master-at-Arms	Brooklyn, N.Y.	Missing
White, John, Landsman	Brooklyn, N.Y.	Injured
White, Robert, Mess Attendant	Portsmouth, Va.	Dead
Whiten, George, Seaman	Middleburg, Va.	Missing
Wickstrom, John, Seaman	Helsingfors, Finland	Missing
Wilbur, Benjamin, Coxswain	Philadelphia, Pa.	Injured
Wilbur, George, Apprentice First Class	Philadelphia, Pa.	Missing
Williams, Henry, Cabin Cook	Richmond, Va.	Injured
Williams, James, Gunner's Mate Third Class	New York City	Injured
Willis, Alonzo, Apprentice Second Class	Keyport, N.J.	Injured
Wills, A. O., Private	Philadelphia, Pa.	Missing
Wilson, Albert, Seaman	Chicago, Ill.	Missing
Wilson, Robert, Chief Quartermaster	New York City	Missing
Ziegler, John, Coal Passer	New Brunswick, N.J.	Missing

Travel Log of the Maine

LEFT	DATE		ARRIVED	DATE	
New York Navy Yard	5 Nov.	'95	Newport, R.I.	16 Nov.	'95
Newport, R.I.	23 Nov.		Portland, Me.	25 Nov.	
Portland, Me.	29 Nov.		Newport, R.I.	30 Nov.	
Newport, R.I.	22 Dec.		Tompkinsville, N.Y.	23 Dec.	
Tompkinsville, N.Y.	24 Dec.		Hampton Roads, Va.*	25 Dec.	
Hampton Roads, Va.	4 June	'96	Key West, Fla.	8 June	'96
Key West, Fla.	30 July		Norfolk, Va.	3 Aug.	
Norfolk, Va.	25 Aug.		Tompkinsville, N.Y.	26 Aug.	
Tompkinsville, N.Y.	1 Sept.		Fishers Island	4 Sept.	
Fishers Island	16 Sept.		Tompkinsville, N.Y.	19 Sept.	
Tompkinsville, N.Y.	1 Oct.		Hampton Roads, Va.	5 Oct.	
Hampton Roads, Va.	12 Oct.		Tompkinsville, N.Y.	14 Oct.	
Tompkinsville, N.Y.	21 Dec.		Hampton Roads, Va.	22 Dec.	
Hampton Roads, Va.	4 Feb.	'97	Charleston, S.C.	8 Feb.	'97

Occasionally such a reference to Hampton Roads includes other places in that general vicinity.

LEFT	DATE	ARRIVED	DATE
Charleston, S.C.	18 Feb.	Port Royal, S.C.	19 Feb.
Port Royal, S.C.	21 Feb.	New Orleans, La.	25 Feb.
New Orleans, La.	11 March	Port Royal, S.C.	15 March
Port Royal, S.C.	3 April	Hampton Roads, Va.	5 April
Hampton Roads, Va.	19 April	Tompkinsville, N.Y.	20 April
Tompkinsville, N.Y.	25 April	North River, N.Y.	25 April
North River, N.Y.	29 April	New York Navy Yard	29 April
New York Navy Yard	23 June	Hampton Roads, Va.	25 June
Hampton Roads, Va.	3 July	New Castle, Del.	5 July
New Castle, Del.	10 July	Tompkinsville, N.Y.	11 July
Tompkinsville, N.Y.	17 July	New London, Conn.	17 July
New London, Conn.	26 July	Fishers Island	26 July
Fishers Island	28 July	Tompkinsville, N.Y.	29 July
Tompkinsville, N.Y.	2 Aug.	Newport, R.I.	3 Aug.
Newport, R.I.	11 Aug.	Portsmouth, N.H.	12 Aug.
Portsmouth, N.H.	16 Aug.	Portland, Me.	16 Aug.
Portland, Me.	24 Aug.	Bar Harbor, Me.	24 Aug.
Bar Harbor, Me.	31 Aug.	Southern Drill Ground	3 Sept.
Southern Drill Ground	12 Sept.	Hampton Roads, Va.	12 Sept.
Hampton Roads, Va.	4 Oct.	Chesapeake Bay	4 Oct.
Chesapeake Bay	5 Oct.	Southern Drill Ground	5 Oct.
Southern Drill Ground	9 Oct.	Port Royal, S.C.	12 Oct.
Port Royal, S.C.	15 Nov.	Hampton Roads, Va.	17 Nov.
Hampton Roads, Va.	11 Dec.	Key West, Fla.	15 Dec.
Key West, Fla.	24 Jan. '98	Dry Tortugas	24 Jan. '98
Dry Tortugas	24 Jan.	Havana, Cuba	25 Jan.

Index

(Complete list of officers and crew appears on pages 183-196)